IS SOLO CONSULTING RIGHT FOR YOU?

A PRACTICAL GUIDE FOR TECHNICAL PROFESSIONALS TO EXPLORE AND LAUNCH AN INDEPENDENT CONSULTING BUSINESS

PHIL CHARLES

GS | GOING SOLO

ALSO BY PHIL CHARLES

Essential Career Skills for Technical Professionals

Master Your Focus Today
Master the Habits of Effective People
The Attention Architect
Why it Matters
The Guide to Accelerating Your Career
How to Do the Hard Things
Focus and Energy Made Easy

Strategy and Planning for Transport Professionals

Addressing Transport Challenges

This book is written using Australain/Brisitish English.

ISBN ebook: 978-1-925996-30-2

ISBN paperback: 978-1-925996-31-9

ISBN hardcover: 978-1-925996-32-6

Published by the Going Solo Academy

https://GoingSolo.Academy

❋ Created with Vellum

CONTENTS

PART 5: PREPARING FOR THE TRANSITION

BONUS FREE RESOURCE

Get a free 7 Day email series, each day with a workbook to develop your Solo Consulting business:

- Day 1. Understanding Solo Consulting
- Day 2. Personal Readiness for Consulting
- Day 3. Market Exploration and Niche Identification
- Day 4. Decision-Making Frameworks
- Day 5. Practical Aspects of Starting a Consulting Business
- Day 6. Creating Your Action Plan
- Day 7. Final Decision and Reflection

Get your free resource now https://bit.ly/solo-consulting

IS SOLO CONSULTING FOR YOU?

Many experienced technical professionals seek more than just being an employee—are you at that career crossroads?

The allure of solo consulting beckons with promises of autonomy, higher income, and meaningful work. Yet, beneath these appealing prospects lie crucial questions that demand answers before making this life-changing leap:

- Can your technical expertise truly translate into a thriving consulting practice?
- How will you replace the security of a steady paycheck?
- Do you have what it takes to run your own business?
- Is the timing right for this transition?

Making the wrong choice could mean years of lost momentum or missing a transformative opportunity. While general consulting advice abounds, technical professionals face unique challenges that generic guidance fails to address.

This book provides a structured, evidence-based framework specifically designed to help you evaluate whether solo consulting aligns with your expertise, goals, and risk tolerance.

Through five carefully crafted parts, you'll gain:

- A clear understanding of what technical consulting really entails, beyond common myths
- A comprehensive self-assessment toolkit calibrated for technical professionals
- Practical strategies to validate market demand for your expertise
- Data-driven frameworks for evaluating risks and opportunities
- A clear path forward, whether consulting is right for you now or not.

This book serves as your personal guide if you:

- Have achieved technical mastery but feel constrained by organisational limits
- Want to leverage your expertise more directly and profitably
- Feel drawn to consulting but hesitate due to uncertainty
- Need a systematic approach to evaluate this career transition
- Seek validation of your consulting potential before making the leap.

Written specifically for technical professionals with over five years of experience, this practical guide helps you avoid costly mistakes and uncover whether solo consulting is your next career move. By the end, you'll have the clarity and confidence to make an informed decision about your professional future.

Take the first step toward clarity regarding your consulting potential. Your career trajectory hinges on making the right choice—make sure it's an informed one.

WHY DID I WRITE THIS BOOK?

I wrote this book based on the lessons I learned from my journey from employee to solo consultant over the past quarter-century. Solo consulting is the best second career for any technical professional. I started by volunteering with a few consultants while still an employee, then joined an international consulting firm, where I felt as though I had dived in at the deep end of the pool before learning to swim!

Moving to an academic position enabled me to start a solo consulting business part-time and eventually transition to full-time. There are many paths you can take, but I recommend beginning by working with another consultant, even on a part-time basis, before making a full-time commitment.

WHY THIS BOOK?

Every day, talented engineers, scientists, and technical professionals stand at a crossroads. The allure of solo consulting promises autonomy and higher income; however, fear often prevents them from leaving a stable career.

Making the wrong choice could mean sacrificing years of career building or missing a life-changing opportunity. While general consulting advice is plentiful, technical professionals face unique challenges that generic guidance fails to address. We understand the weight of this decision: you've invested years in building technical expertise in a structured environment.

The questions weighing on you are real:
Will my technical skills translate to consulting?
How do I replace the security of a steady salary?
Can I handle the business side of consulting?

Whether you're a seasoned engineer feeling constrained by an organisational hierarchy, a technologist seeking more project diversity, or a scientist exploring ways to maximise your impact, these concerns resonate across the technical community.

The cost of uncertainty in this decision is substantial. Many technical professionals either:

- Leap without proper preparation, learning expensive lessons through trial and error
- Remain stuck in unfulfilling roles, watching opportunities pass by
- Follow generic consulting advice that doesn't address the unique challenges of technical consulting
- Struggle to validate their market value, leading to underpricing or misaligned services.

Without a structured approach to this decision, you risk missing your optimal career path or starting your consulting journey on shaky ground.

This book provides a systematic, evidence-based approach to help you evaluate whether solo consulting aligns with your expertise, goals, and risk tolerance. Unlike generic consulting guides, it is specifically designed for technical professionals, offering:

- A structured framework for decision-making that appeals to analytical minds
- Self-assessment tools calibrated for technical expertise
- Market validation strategies to test your consulting potential
- Risk-mitigation approaches for a potential transition.

HOW THE BOOK DELIVERS:

Through five carefully structured parts, this book guides you through a systematic evaluation process:

Part 1: Understanding the World of Solo Consulting. This section dispels the myths and misconceptions surrounding technical consulting, offering a clear perspective on what successful solo consultants actually do. You will gain insight into the various consulting models available to technical professionals and how these correspond with different levels of expertise and work preferences.

Part 2: Self-Assessment: Are You Ready for Consulting? This section provides practical tools for evaluating your technical, business, and interpersonal readiness for consulting. Using proven assessment frameworks, you will identify your strengths, weaknesses, and areas requiring development before making the transition.

Part 3: Exploring the Market and Identifying Your Niche. This section teaches you how to validate market demand for your expertise and find your optimal consulting niche. It includes methods for testing your market assumptions and identifying high-value opportunities within your technical domain.

Part 4: Decision-Making: Is Solo Consulting Right for You? This section offers a data-driven approach to weigh your options. It features decision matrices and risk assessment tools tailored for technical professionals. You will gain a clear understanding of whether consulting aligns with your career goals and personal circumstances.

Part 5: Preparing for the Transition. This section outlines the initial steps for a successful transition for those who choose to proceed. It emphasises essential mindset shifts, preliminary planning, and network activation.

Each section builds on the previous one, creating a comprehensive evaluation framework to help you make an informed decision about your consulting future.

WHO THIS BOOK IS FOR

This book serves technical professionals at critical career decision points, specifically:

- Mid to late-career technical professionals who have built substantial expertise but feel constrained by traditional employment

- Technical experts seeking greater control over their professional impact
- Professionals with 5-7+ years of experience who have accumulated deep domain knowledge in their field
- Those already doing occasional consulting work who are considering a full-time transition.

You Will Find This Book Particularly Valuable if You:

- Have achieved technical mastery but feel that your growth is plateauing
- Want to leverage your expertise more directly and profitably
- Feel drawn to consulting but hesitate due to uncertainty about the business aspects
- Need a systematic approach to evaluate this career transition
- Are looking for validation of your consulting potential before making the leap.

This Book May Not Be For You If:

- You are early in your technical career with limited hands-on experience
- You are seeking immediate 'how-to' guidance on setting up a consulting business
- You are primarily interested in joining an established consulting firm
- You are seeking quick answers without engaging in deep self-assessment.

The focus of this book is on helping experienced technical professionals make informed decisions about solo consulting. It employs frameworks and approaches that resonate with analytical minds.

MAKING THE MOST OF THIS BOOK

To maximise your return on investment in this decision-making process, consider this book a systematic evaluation framework rather than merely an informational resource.

Key Concepts

Each chapter in this book concludes with a "Key Concepts" section that distils the 20% of insights that deliver 80% of the value. Think of it as a practical checklist or a quick reminder of the chapter's most important takeaways. These summaries are designed to help you:

- **Reinforce Your Learning**: Quickly revisit and retain the chapter's essential ideas without having to reread everything.
- **Apply Concepts Practically**: Use the key points as a guide to evaluate your readiness, identify priorities, and plan actionable next steps.
- **Stay Focused**: When making decisions about your consulting journey, refer back to these summaries to remain aligned with your goals and the realities of consulting.

Whether you're deciding if consulting is right for you or refining your approach, these "Key Concepts" provide a roadmap for confidently navigating the challenges and opportunities of solo consulting.

INTRODUCING AI PROMPTS FOR REFLECTION AND PERSONALISATION

Consulting is a deeply personal journey, and no two paths look the same. "AI Reflection Prompts" have been included at the end of most sections to help you explore how the concepts in each chapter apply to your unique situation. These prompts are designed to encourage self-reflection, spark ideas, and guide you in taking actionable steps tailored to your goals, lifestyle, and aspirations. Complete the prompts in a single chat, as this will provide a growing context of your background, skills, and interests.

If you prefer not to use AI, feel free to use the prompts as reflection questions.

Whether you journal your responses, discuss them with a mentor, or use them to inform your next steps, these prompts will help you connect the chapter's ideas to your consulting practice and ensure they resonate with your personal vision. By engaging with the prompts, you can gain clarity, strengthen your plan, and take ownership of your consulting journey.

RECOMMENDED APPROACH:

Sequential Progress

- Work through the chapters in order—each one builds on the previous concepts
- Complete all assessments and exercises before moving forward
- Document your insights and concerns in a dedicated decision journal
- Revisit earlier chapters as new questions arise.

Practical Application

- Treat the self-assessment tools like technical evaluations—be thorough and objective
- Use the provided exercises to assess your readiness across different dimensions
- Track your confidence levels regarding consulting as you progress through each section
- Document specific questions or concerns that require further investigation.

Decision Support Tools

- Leverage the included decision tools to evaluate options systematically

- Use the risk assessment frameworks to identify and assess potential challenges
- Apply the market validation tools to test your assumptions
- Track your progress using the readiness checklist provided at each milestone.

Engagement Strategies

- Set aside dedicated time for reflection after each chapter
- Share insights with trusted mentors or colleagues who have made similar transitions
- Keep a running list of action items that emerge from your reading
- Note specific areas where you need more data or clarity.

Expected Outcomes:

By fully engaging with this book, you should:

- Gain clarity about your consulting readiness
- Develop a data-backed decision about your next career move
- Identify specific areas requiring development
- Create an initial action plan, whether moving toward consulting or strengthening your current position.

The goal isn't to push you toward consulting but to help you make an informed decision about your professional future.

This structured approach ensures you reach an analytically sound and personally confident decision, regardless of your chosen path.

Welcome to *Is Solo Consulting Right for Me?* Let's begin this journey together.

PART 1: UNDERSTANDING THE WORLD OF SOLO CONSULTING

The best way to predict your future is to create it.

PETER DRUCKER

1: WHAT IS SOLO CONSULTING?

Solo consulting conjures images of freedom—freedom from office politics, the freedom to choose projects, and the freedom to work on your terms. While these perceptions hold true, the reality of solo consulting is nuanced and varied.

This chapter will explore what solo consulting entails, its different forms, and how it contrasts with traditional employment in technical fields.

1.1 DEFINING SOLO CONSULTING

At its core, solo consulting involves offering your expertise as an independent professional to clients who require it but may lack the necessary internal skills or the capacity to hire a full-time expert.

Consultants are brought in to solve specific problems, provide strategic advice, or temporarily lend their technical skills to projects.

Unlike traditional employment, where you work for one employer, consultants typically juggle multiple clients and projects, creating a diversified work experience. Solo consulting is distinct from working within a consulting firm; as a solo consultant, you operate as a one-person business.

This means you are responsible for delivering on your projects, finding clients, managing your business operations, setting your rates, and handling your marketing and finances.

While larger firms provide a buffer of support and a steady workflow, solo consultants thrive on independence and self-reliance.

There are various models of solo consulting, including:

- **Freelance Consulting:** Typically project-based, you are hired for a specific task or project. This is common in software development, data analysis, engineering design, and project management.
- **Contract Consulting:** These longer-term engagements resemble traditional employment but have defined start and end dates. Contract consultants usually work on-site with clients and are embedded within teams.
- **Advisory or Strategic Consulting:** In this model, you provide technical advice and strategic direction. This is common among experienced professionals who guide decision-making processes without involvement in day-to-day operations.

Each model has its own dynamics, and understanding which aligns with your skills and preferences is part of determining whether consulting is right for you.

AI Reflection Prompts: *What does solo consulting mean for someone with my expertise and background? [provide a brief background of your expertise] Can you outline how it might differ from working within a consulting firm?*

Which consulting model—freelance, contract, or advisory—might best suit my skills, preferences, and career goals? Can you explain why? [provide a brief outline of your skills, preferences, and career goals]

1.2 THE INDEPENDENCE FACTOR

One of the most appealing aspects of solo consulting is independence. As a solo consultant, you can choose the projects you want to work on, set your schedule, and decide where and how you work. This independence is a powerful draw for many technical professionals, especially if they have spent years in structured environments with rigid hierarchies.

However, independence comes with its own set of challenges. While you are free from the oversight of a boss, you are also without the support of a structured team. Decisions about project scope, deadlines, and deliverables rest squarely on your shoulders. Independence means that self-motivation is crucial—you set the pace and are accountable for meeting client expectations.

Independence in consulting also means handling the business side. Beyond delivering expert advice or technical solutions, you will need to manage contracts, invoices, and payments. The allure of independence is real, but it is balanced by the necessity to be disciplined and proactive in running your business.

> **AI Reflection Prompt:** *How can I evaluate my suitability for the independence and self-motivation required in consulting? Can you suggest some practical ways to prepare for this?*

1.3 HOW SOLO CONSULTING DIFFERS FROM TRADITIONAL EMPLOYMENT

For technical professionals, the shift from traditional employment to solo consulting represents a fundamental change in how work is experienced. Here are some key differences:

- **Job Security vs. Client Pipeline:** Traditional employment offers stability—a steady paycheck, benefits, and a defined role. In consulting, your income depends on your ability to find and secure clients. The *job security* of consulting is built on your network, the outcomes you produce, your reputation, and the demand for your expertise.

- **Specialisation vs. Breadth of Skills:** In a traditional job, your role is often specialised, allowing you to focus deeply on one area. Consulting, however, requires a broader set of skills. You need your technical expertise and skills in project management, client communication, negotiation, marketing, and sales.

- **Defined Structure vs. Flexibility:** Employment in technical fields typically involves working within established structures —teams, departments, and organisational hierarchies. Consulting offers flexibility in how you structure your work, but it also means you must create your own processes and systems.

- **Steady Routine vs. Variable Workload:** Traditional jobs have a predictable routine. Consulting can be cyclical, with periods of intense work followed by slower times. This variability can be beneficial (providing more control over one's time) and challenging (introducing income instability).

AI Reflection Prompt: *Based on my current role [insert role], can you help me compare consulting and traditional employment regarding job security, variety, and flexibility?*

1.4 THE ROLE OF EXPERTISE IN CONSULTING

Consulting relies heavily on your ability to offer specialised knowledge and solve problems that clients need to address. Your specialised technical skills and experience are your primary assets. However, consulting also places a premium on how well you can communicate that expertise and translate it into solutions that deliver results.

It is not enough to be knowledgeable; you must also be able to apply your knowledge to create solutions for your clients. In consulting, your value is tied to the impact you can create. This might involve improving a client's process efficiency, providing innovative solutions to complex problems, or helping a company navigate technical challenges that they lack the in-house capability to handle.

Your ability to clearly define and articulate your value proposition is crucial; it is how you differentiate yourself in the market and attract clients. Successful consultants blend deep expertise with skills to listen, ask the right questions, and align their solutions with their clients' goals. Consulting can be rewarding if you enjoy problem-solving and find value in sharing your expertise to make a tangible impact.

> **AI Reflection Prompt:** *What steps can I take to define and articulate my value proposition as a consultant clearly? How can I communicate the impact of my expertise to potential clients?*

1.5 UNDERSTANDING THE COMMITMENT OF CONSULTING

Recognising that consulting is a commitment, not just a job, is important. When you enter the consulting world, you are committing to being a business owner, with all the responsibilities that come with it.

This means being prepared for business development, client management, and staying current in your field. Consulting requires a proactive mindset—clients will not come to you simply because you have decided to start consulting.

Building and maintaining a pipeline of work requires continuous effort, time, strategy, and persistence. The commitment to consulting is balanced by your control over your professional career, making it worthwhile when you are ready to embrace the challenges and rewards.

Solo consulting offers a unique and dynamic career path for technical professionals, characterised by independence, diverse work, and the opportunity to leverage your expertise in impactful ways.

However, it also demands self-reliance, adaptability, and a willingness to manage the uncertainties of running a business. As you read this book, remember the foundational elements of consulting outlined in this chapter; they are the building blocks for understanding whether this path is right for you.

AI Reflection Prompts: *What does it mean to fully commit to consulting as a career? Can you help me identify the key mindset shifts I need to make as I transition from employment?*

What are the most significant challenges of solo consulting for someone like me, and how might I address them while making the most of its opportunities?

KEY CONCEPTS

Solo consulting offers independence, diverse work, and impactful opportunities. However, it also demands self-reliance, adaptability, and strong business management skills. Thus, it is a rewarding path for technical professionals ready to commit to a dynamic career.

1.1 Defining Solo Consulting

Solo consulting involves offering expertise as an independent professional to solve specific problems or provide strategic advice.

Consultants work with multiple clients, unlike traditional employees, who serve a single employer.

Solo consulting differs from firm-based consulting: you handle all aspects of business operations, from client acquisition to finances.

Common models of solo consulting:

Freelance Consulting: Short-term, project-based work.

Contract Consulting: Longer-term, embedded engagements with a defined timeframe.

Advisory/Strategic Consulting: High-level advice without daily operational involvement.

1.2 The Independence Factor

Independence allows consultants to choose projects, set schedules, and control their work environment.

Independence requires self-motivation, discipline, and accountability.

Beyond technical work, solo consultants manage business aspects, including contracts, invoices, and marketing.

1.3 How Solo Consulting Differs from Traditional Employment

Job Security vs. Client Pipeline: Stability in employment contrasts with the need to maintain a steady stream of clients in consulting.

Specialisation vs. Breadth of Skills: Consultants require deep technical expertise and broader business skills (e.g., communication, sales, and project management).

Defined Structure vs. Flexibility: Employment provides clear structures; consulting requires creating personal workflows and systems.

Steady Routine vs. Variable Workload: Consulting involves fluctuating workloads, offering flexibility but less income predictability.

1.4 The Role of Expertise in Consulting

Success hinges on leveraging technical expertise to solve client problems and deliver tangible results.

Communication and problem-solving are as crucial as technical skills; clients value the clear articulation of solutions and results.

A strong value proposition helps attract clients and differentiate yourself in the market.

Impact-driven consulting involves aligning solutions with client goals, whether improving efficiency or resolving technical challenges.

1.5 Understanding the Commitment of Consulting

Consulting requires a long-term commitment to business ownership and requires continuous learning, networking, and client acquisition.

Building a sustainable pipeline of work necessitates ongoing strategy, persistence, and adaptability.

The balance of challenges and rewards makes consulting worthwhile for those willing to embrace its entrepreneurial nature.

EXERCISE

Complete the *Self-Assessment Quiz* below.

This assessment complements the content of the book, helping you gauge your readiness and interest in pursuing solo consulting. It will allow you to:

- Evaluate your strengths and areas for growth in consulting
- Gain clarity on your suitability for solo consulting
- Reflect on key areas such as independence, client management, and business skills.

SELF-ASSESSMENT QUIZ: MEASURING READINESS FOR SOLO CONSULTING

Self-assessment is a critical first step for anyone considering the transition to solo consulting. It provides a structured way to evaluate your readiness, strengths, and areas for improvement. By reflecting on your current mindset, skills, and resources, you can clarify whether this path aligns with your personal and professional goals.

This exercise is not about passing or failing; it's about creating self-awareness. A clear understanding of your readiness will empower you to take actionable steps to prepare for a successful consulting journey.

Overview of the Self-Assessment Tool

The self-assessment tool is designed to evaluate your readiness across four key areas:

Instructions:

Answer each question honestly based on your current skills, mindset, and situation. Use the scoring guide at the end to interpret your results. Rate each statement on a scale of 1 to 5, where 1 means Strongly Disagree, 3 means Neutral, and 5 means Strongly Agree.

. . .

Section 1: Personal Readiness

1. I am comfortable working independently and making my own decisions.
2. I am willing to take calculated risks, including financial uncertainty.
3. I am self-disciplined and can manage my time effectively without external oversight.
4. I am resilient and can handle setbacks or rejection.
5. I am motivated to learn and continuously improve my skills.

Section 2: Professional Readiness

6. I have deep technical expertise that provides value to potential clients.
7. I can clearly articulate my skills and the unique value I offer.
8. I have experience solving specific problems for clients or employers.
9. I am comfortable engaging with clients, including networking, pitching, and building relationships.
10. I am confident in adapting my expertise to fit different projects or industries.

Section 3: Business Readiness

11. I understand that running a consulting business requires managing finances, contracts, and marketing.
12. I am comfortable with tasks such as negotiating rates, handling contracts, and invoicing.
13. I am prepared to spend time finding clients and building a pipeline of work.
14. I can manage income variability and plan for lean periods.
15. I have a financial cushion or safety net to support me during the initial transition.

Section 4: Lifestyle Fit

16. I value flexibility in my work schedule and can balance it with personal responsibilities.
17. I have the support of family, friends, or a professional network in pursuing solo consulting.
18. I am willing to trade stability for autonomy in my work life.
19. I am comfortable with a non-traditional career structure.
20. I have considered how solo consulting aligns with my personal values and goals.

Scoring and Interpretation

Step 1: Calculate Your Total Score. Add up the scores for all 20 questions.

Step 2: Interpret Your Results

- **80-100** (High Readiness): You are well-prepared to transition into solo consulting. Focus on refining your goals and taking actionable steps to launch your business.
- **60-79** (Moderate Readiness): You possess many strengths, but to feel fully ready, you may need to address specific areas, such as financial planning or building a network.
- **40-59** (Low Readiness): You may not yet be fully prepared for solo consulting. Before proceeding, identify areas for improvement and concentrate on skill-building, financial preparation, or mindset shifts.
- **Below 40** (Not Ready Yet): Solo consulting may not align with your current skills, mindset, or situation. After addressing significant gaps, consider revisiting this option.

Step 3: Analyse Your Results. Once you complete the assessment, take time to analyse your results:

Strengths: In which areas did you score the highest? These are the skills and traits you can leverage immediately.

Gaps: In which areas did you score the lowest? Identify specific actions to address these gaps, such as building financial resilience or improving client engagement skills.

Patterns: Do your results align with your self-perception? Are there any surprises?

Step 4. Reflection. Reflect on these questions to deepen your under-standing of your assessment results:

1. What surprised you about your self-assessment results?
2. In which areas did you score the lowest, and why do you think that is?
3. What specific steps can you take to improve in those areas?
4. What strengths do you feel most confident about leveraging in your consulting journey?

Write down your reflections and revisit them as you progress through this course. They will serve as a roadmap for your growth.

2: THE REWARDS AND CHALLENGES OF CONSULTING

S olo consulting is often portrayed as the ultimate career freedom—no bosses, no office politics, and the ability to choose projects that excite you.

While these aspects are certainly enticing, the reality of consulting is more nuanced. Understanding the rewards and challenges of consulting is essential for making an informed decision about whether this path is right for you.

This chapter explores the benefits that draw many technical professionals to consulting, as well as the potential pitfalls and challenges accompanying it. Examining both sides will give you a balanced view of what consulting entails.

2.1 THE REWARDS OF SOLO CONSULTING

For many technical professionals, the rewards of solo consulting extend beyond financial gains. The appeal often lies in the lifestyle changes and personal fulfilment that consulting can offer. Let's take a closer look at some of the most significant benefits:

Independence and Control

One of the primary draws of solo consulting is the independence it offers. As a consultant, you have the autonomy to set your schedule, choose the projects you work on, and make decisions without having to navigate corporate hierarchies or seek approval from multiple levels of management.

This control over your professional life allows you to align your work with your values, interests, and long-term goals. Independence also means you can shape your work environment and processes to suit your personal preferences.

Whether you thrive in a home office, prefer working from coffee shops, or enjoy travelling and working remotely, consulting gives you the flexibility to design your ideal work setup.

This freedom appeals to those who have spent years in rigid work environments with little room for personal choice.

Variety of Projects and Continuous Learning

Solo consulting offers the opportunity to work on a diverse range of projects. Instead of being tied to a single role or department, you can engage with different clients across various industries, each bringing new challenges and learning opportunities.

This variety keeps your work interesting and accelerates your professional growth.

You're constantly exposed to new problems, technologies, and methodologies, which can be highly stimulating and rewarding for those who love to learn and adapt.

Choosing projects that align with your passions and expertise allows you to focus on work that truly excites you.

For many consultants, the most rewarding aspect of their career is the chance to make a meaningful impact by solving complex problems that matter to them and their clients.

Potential for Higher Earnings

Consulting can offer significant earning potential, especially for those with specialised skills in high demand. As a consultant, you can set your rates, which may be considerably higher than a traditional salary, particularly when working on high-stakes projects or with clients who urgently require your unique expertise.

Furthermore, the ability to take on multiple clients means that your income is not capped as it might be in a traditional job.

However, it is important to note that higher earnings are not guaranteed. They often result from effective business development, strong client relationships, and consistently delivering high value.

While consulting offers the potential for greater financial rewards, it also requires a proactive approach to securing work and managing finances.

Personal Fulfilment and Work-Life Balance

Many consultants find that controlling their workload and schedule leads to greater personal fulfilment and a better work-life balance.

Unlike traditional employment, where company demands largely dictate your time, consulting lets you decide when and how much you work.

This flexibility enables you to better balance professional responsibilities with personal commitments, hobbies, or even additional entrepreneurial ventures.

For those who value time with family, pursuing personal interests, or simply having the freedom to take breaks when needed, consulting offers a level of flexibility that is hard to match in conventional roles.

One of the most rewarding aspects of consulting is the personal fulfilment that comes from controlling your career and working in alignment with your values.

AI Reflection Prompts: *How can I make the most of the independence and flexibility that consulting offers while staying productive and focused?*

What strategies can I use to maximise my earning potential in consulting while managing income variability?

2.2 THE CHALLENGES OF SOLO CONSULTING

While the rewards of consulting are compelling, it is equally important to consider the challenges.

Consulting has its pitfalls, and understanding these challenges is crucial for anyone considering this path. Let us explore some of the most common hurdles consultants face:

Income Variability and Financial Uncertainty

One of the most significant challenges of solo consulting is income variability.

Unlike a traditional job with a steady paycheck, consulting income can fluctuate greatly from month to month. Projects may end unexpectedly, clients may delay payments, or work can dry up during slower seasons. This financial uncertainty requires consultants to be adept at budgeting, saving, and managing cash flow to ensure stability, even when business is slow.

Building a pipeline of steady work is an ongoing effort that involves marketing, networking, and occasionally accepting projects that are less than ideal just to keep the income flowing.

This variability can be a major adjustment for those accustomed to the financial security of regular employment. It is essential to have a financial buffer and a clear plan for managing lean periods to navigate the ups and downs of consulting.

Client Acquisition and Management

Finding and retaining clients is another critical challenge in solo consulting. Unlike in a traditional job where work is assigned, consultants must constantly seek out new opportunities. This involves marketing services, building relationships, and negotiating contracts.

Client acquisition can be time-consuming and often involves dealing with rejection or competition from other consultants.

Once you have clients, managing them effectively is a distinct skill. This includes setting clear expectations, maintaining communication, and sometimes navigating difficult situations such as scope creep or disagreements over deliverables.

Successful consultants balance their technical skills with strong interpersonal abilities, managing client relationships to ensure satisfaction and repeat business.

Balancing Multiple Roles

As a solo consultant, you wear many hats. In addition to delivering core consulting services, you are responsible for sales, marketing, finance, project management, and administrative tasks. This can be overwhelming, especially for those accustomed to having dedicated support teams in a traditional work setting.

The challenge of balancing these multiple roles requires effective time management and the ability to prioritise tasks.

It also involves knowing when to delegate or outsource certain aspects of your business, such as accounting or marketing, to free up time for higher-value activities.

Being a jack-of-all-trades is a common reality in consulting, and it is important to be prepared for the breadth of responsibilities that come with running your own business.

Isolation and Lack of Team Support

Another often overlooked challenge of solo consulting is the potential for isolation. Working independently means missing out on the camaraderie, collaboration, and immediate feedback that comes from being part of a team. While solitude is a welcome change for some, it can also be a significant drawback for others.

Without colleagues to bounce ideas off or a team to share the workload, consultants must be self-sufficient and find alternative ways to stay connected.

This might include joining professional networks, attending industry events, or participating in online communities of like-minded professionals. Building a support system is essential to counteract the isolation that can accompany solo consulting.

Managing Self-Motivation and Discipline

Consulting requires a high level of self-motivation and discipline. With no boss to hold you accountable, it is up to you to set deadlines, stay organised, and ensure that projects are completed on time.

This self-directed approach can be liberating, but it demands a strong work ethic and the ability to stay focused without external pressure. Procrastination, distractions, and the temptation to take too much time off can all undermine productivity and impact business success.

Developing routines, setting goals, and maintaining a clear vision for your consulting practice is crucial for staying on track and achieving your professional objectives.

> **AI Reflection Prompts:** *How can I develop a reliable process for finding clients, building relationships, and retaining them over time?*
>
> *How can I address potential feelings of isolation in consulting, and what strategies can I use to stay connected to a supportive network?*

2.3 A BALANCED VIEW: WEIGHING THE REWARDS AND CHALLENGES

Deciding whether solo consulting is the right path requires weighing these rewards and challenges against your professional goals, personal preferences, and risk tolerance. The independence, variety, and potential for higher earnings make consulting attractive for many technical professionals.

However, the realities of income variability, client management, and the need for self-discipline highlight the importance of being prepared for the less glamorous aspects of consulting. Ultimately, the decision to pursue consulting should be based on a realistic understanding of the benefits and challenges.

Consulting can be incredibly rewarding for those ready to embrace its demands, but it is not a one-size-fits-all solution. By carefully considering the factors outlined in this chapter, you can better gauge whether the rewards of consulting align with your aspirations and whether you are prepared to navigate the challenges that come with it.

Solo consulting offers a unique blend of independence, variety, and personal fulfilment, making it appealing to many technical professionals.

However, it also comes with significant challenges, including financial uncertainty, the need for self-management, and the responsibility of juggling multiple roles.

As you continue exploring whether consulting is the right path for you, consider these rewards and challenges and how they align with your career goals and personal values.

KEY CONCEPTS

Solo consulting offers a unique combination of independence, variety, and personal fulfilment but necessitates careful navigation of financial uncertainty, client management, and self-discipline. Understanding both the rewards and challenges is essential for determining whether this path aligns with your career aspirations and personal values.

2.1 The Rewards of Solo Consulting

Independence and Control: Autonomy to set your schedule, choose projects, and make decisions without navigating corporate hierarchies.

Freedom in Work Setup: Flexibility to create a work environment tailored to personal preferences, such as remote work or travel.

Variety of Projects: Exposure to diverse industries and challenges fosters continuous learning and keeps work engaging.

Opportunity for Continuous Growth: Constantly encountering new problems, technologies, and methodologies accelerates professional development.

Potential for Higher Earnings: If managed effectively, the ability to set your rates and take on multiple clients can lead to significant financial rewards.

Personal Fulfilment: Aligning your work with your values and interests enhances career satisfaction.

Work-Life Balance: Control over workload and schedule allows for greater flexibility to prioritise family, hobbies, and personal commitments.

2.2 The Challenges of Solo Consulting

Income Variability: Unpredictable earnings due to fluctuating workloads, project delays, or slow business periods. This requires strong budgeting and financial planning.

Client Acquisition and Management: Marketing services, building relationships, and negotiating contracts are time-intensive and often competitive.

Balancing Multiple Roles: Solo consultants must handle all business functions, from sales and marketing to finance and administration.

Isolation: The lack of team support and camaraderie can lead to feelings of loneliness. Networking and community involvement are vital for connection.

Self-Motivation and Discipline: Success depends on staying organised, setting goals, and avoiding procrastination without external oversight.

Navigating Scope Creep: It is frequently challenging to manage client expectations and deliverables to prevent projects from exceeding agreed-upon terms.

2.3 A Balanced View: Weighing Rewards and Challenges

Alignment with Goals and Values: Consulting offers independence, variety, and potential fulfilment but demands adaptability, discipline, and risk tolerance.

Preparation is Key: Financial planning, self-management skills, and a realistic understanding of the challenges increase the likelihood of success.

Not for Everyone: While rewarding, solo consulting requires you to embrace its benefits and inherent difficulties.

REFLECTION

Examine the potential benefits and challenges of consulting and consider how they might impact you personally.

1. *Which potential rewards of consulting resonate most with you, and how do they align with your goals?*
2. *What consulting challenges are you most concerned about, and how might you address or prepare for these challenges?*

3: CONSULTING MYTHS AND MISCONCEPTIONS

When considering a transition to solo consulting, it's easy to be swayed by success stories and the allure of autonomy. However, the consulting world is often surrounded by myths and misconceptions that can lead to unrealistic expectations.

In this chapter, we debunk some of the most common myths about consulting, helping you build a clearer, more accurate picture of what it truly involves. By addressing these misconceptions, you will be better equipped to decide if consulting is a realistic and suitable career choice.

3.1 MYTH #1: CONSULTING IS AN EASY WAY TO MAKE MONEY

One of the most pervasive myths about consulting is that it is a fast track to high earnings with minimal effort. The image of consultants charging high hourly rates and raking in significant profits creates the impression that consulting is a straightforward path to financial success. While it is true that consulting can offer lucrative opportunities, the reality is far more complex. Consulting is a business; like any business, it requires effort, strategy, and persistence.

High earnings in consulting are often the result of years of experience, a well-established reputation, and a strong network of clients. Despite significant expertise, consultants must continually market their services, negotiate contracts, and manage client relationships.

The income potential is there, but it is closely tied to your ability to deliver value, differentiate yourself in the market, and maintain a steady pipeline of work.

Additionally, consulting comes with financial risks not present in traditional employment. Without the safety net of a regular paycheck, consultants must manage the unpredictability of client work, project delays, and payment issues. Financial success in consulting requires careful planning, strong business acumen, and a willingness to navigate the ups and downs of self-employment.

> **AI Reflection Prompt:** *What are the common misconceptions about the financial rewards of consulting, and how can I realistically evaluate my earning potential as a consultant?*

3.2 MYTH #2: CONSULTING IS ONLY FOR EXTROVERTS AND BUSINESS-SAVVY INDIVIDUALS

Another common misconception is that consulting is only suitable for outgoing, business-savvy individuals who excel in networking and self-promotion. This myth can be particularly discouraging for technical professionals who may view themselves as more introverted or who lack formal business training.

The truth is that consulting is about leveraging your expertise to solve problems, and success is not limited to one personality type. While networking and client engagement are important aspects of consulting, many successful consultants are introverts who have found ways to connect with clients that suit their style.

For example, introverts often excel at one-on-one interactions, deep listening, and thoughtful problem-solving—skills that are highly valued in consulting. Similarly, while having business knowledge is beneficial, it is not a prerequisite for starting a consulting practice.

Many technical professionals transition into consulting with little business experience and learn as they go. There are numerous resources available, from online courses to mentorship programs, that can help you build the necessary business skills. Consulting is not about fitting a specific mould; it's about finding a way to use your strengths to add value to clients.

> **AI Reflection Prompt:** *How can someone with an introverted personality or limited business experience succeed as a consultant? What steps should I take to prepare?*

3.3 MYTH #3: CONSULTANTS HAVE COMPLETE CONTROL OVER THEIR TIME

One of the major draws of consulting is the idea of complete control over your schedule, which is a myth that can lead to disappointment. While consulting does offer more flexibility than a traditional job, client demands and project deadlines often dictate how you spend your time.

Clients expect results; you are accountable for meeting those expectations as a consultant. This can mean working late nights and weekends or adjusting your schedule to accommodate client needs, especially when juggling multiple projects.

While you may be able to take time off between projects, taking a break also means pausing your income stream, which can add pressure to secure the next contract quickly. Furthermore, managing your time effectively is crucial to maintaining a consulting business. Beyond client work, you'll need to allocate time for business development, administrative tasks, and continuous learning to keep your skills relevant. The promise of complete time freedom is tempered by the realities of running a business and meeting client obligations.

> **AI Reflection Prompt:** *How can I set realistic expectations for managing my time as a consultant and balance flexibility with client demands?*

3.4 MYTH #4: CONSULTING IS JUST ABOUT GIVING ADVICE

A common misconception is that consulting is merely about giving advice. Instead, consultants spend their days offering recommendations while also getting involved in implementation.

While advisory roles exist, most consulting engagements require a hands-on approach. Clients hire consultants to solve problems, which often involves rolling up your sleeves and engaging in the practical aspects of a project.

Consultants are expected to provide strategic guidance and contribute directly to project execution. This could involve analysing data, developing solutions, or implementing recommendations alongside a client's team.

The ability to bridge the gap between strategy and execution is one of the key skills that differentiates successful consultants.

Additionally, consulting requires more than just technical expertise. You will need to manage client expectations, navigate organisational dynamics, and adapt your approach as projects evolve.

The role of a consultant is multifaceted, and success depends on your ability to move seamlessly between advising, executing, and managing client relationships.

> **AI Reflection Prompt:** *How can I prepare for the practical, hands-on aspects of consulting beyond giving strategic advice?*

3.5 MYTH #5: CONSULTING OFFERS IMMEDIATE VALIDATION AND RECOGNITION

Another myth is that consulting will bring immediate recognition and validation for your expertise.

Building credibility as a consultant takes time. Unlike traditional employment, where one's role and contributions are often recognised within the organisation, consultants must continually prove their value to each new client.

Establishing a strong reputation involves consistently delivering results, building client trust, and earning referrals and testimonials.

Early in your consulting career, you may need to take on smaller projects or work at lower rates to build your portfolio and demonstrate your capabilities. Recognition in consulting comes from a track record of success, requiring patience and persistence.

Moreover, consulting can sometimes be a solitary pursuit without the built-in feedback mechanisms of a traditional job.

Consultants must be comfortable with self-assessment and actively seek client feedback to refine their approach.

The validation in consulting is often more nuanced and must be earned through the outcomes you deliver rather than through formal accolades or promotions.

> **AI Reflection Prompt:** *What strategies can I use to build credibility and earn recognition as a new consultant, even without a long track record?*

3.6 A BALANCED PERSPECTIVE ON CONSULTING MYTHS

The myths surrounding consulting can create a skewed perception of the career. It is important to approach consulting with realistic expectations, understanding that while the rewards are significant, they come with their own set of challenges.

By debunking these myths, we aim to provide a clearer view of the consulting landscape, helping you make a more informed decision about whether this path aligns with your goals and strengths.

Consulting is not a magic solution or an easy escape from the constraints of traditional employment. It is a career path that requires resilience, adaptability, and a willingness to embrace the uncertainties and opportunities it presents.

Success in consulting is not about fitting a particular mould but about leveraging your unique skills and experiences to create value for your clients.

This chapter provides a more realistic picture of a career in consulting by addressing common myths and misconceptions about it.

Consulting offers a unique blend of independence, variety, and the opportunity to make a meaningful impact. However, it also requires careful consideration of the challenges involved, as well as a commitment to continuous learning and adaptation.

As you continue exploring consulting, consider these myths and seek out information that will help you develop a clear and balanced understanding of the field.

> **AI Reflection Prompt:** *What strategies can I use to build credibility and earn recognition as a new consultant, even without a long track record?*

KEY CONCEPTS

Debunking common consulting myths provides a realistic view of the profession. While consulting offers independence, variety, and meaningful work, it demands financial planning, adaptability, and the ability to manage multiple roles effectively. Understanding these realities helps you make an informed decision about whether consulting aligns with your goals and strengths.

3.1 Myth #1: Consulting is an Easy Way to Make Money

High earnings in consulting are not guaranteed; they require effort, strategy, and persistence.

Financial success is tied to delivering value, differentiating yourself, and maintaining a steady client pipeline.

Consulting involves financial risks, including unpredictable income, project delays, and payment issues.

Success demands careful financial planning, business acumen, and resilience.

3.2 Myth #2: Consulting is Only for Extroverts and Business-Savvy Individuals

Success in consulting is not limited to extroverts; introverts often excel in one-on-one interactions, deep listening, and problem-solving.

Business knowledge is helpful but not essential; many consultants learn necessary skills through experience, mentorship, and online resources.

Consulting is about leveraging your expertise, rather than fitting a specific personality type.

3.3 Myth #3: Consultants Have Complete Control Over Their Time

While consulting offers flexibility, client demands and deadlines often dictate your schedule.

Time off between projects pauses income, adding pressure to secure new contracts.

Time management is critical for balancing client work, business development, and administrative tasks.

True "time freedom" is tempered by the responsibilities of running a business.

3.4 Myth #4: Consulting is Just About Giving Advice

Consulting often involves hands-on problem-solving and implementation, not just offering recommendations.

Successful consultants bridge the gap between strategy and execution.

Managing client expectations, navigating organisational dynamics, and adapting to project changes are key elements of consulting.

A multifaceted role requires balancing advisory work, execution, and relationship management.

3.5 Myth #5: Consulting Offers Immediate Validation and Recognition

Building credibility as a consultant takes time and effort; the early stages may involve smaller projects or lower rates.

Recognition in consulting comes from delivering results, earning client trust, and securing referrals and testimonials.

Feedback mechanisms are less structured than in traditional employment; therefore, consultants must actively seek feedback and engage in self-assessment.

Validation comes from the impact of your work rather than from formal accolades or promotions.

3.6 A Balanced Perspective on Consulting Myths

Myths about consulting can create unrealistic expectations, leading to disappointment if not addressed.

Consulting offers significant rewards, such as independence and the opportunity to make an impact, but it also comes with challenges that require resilience and adaptability.

Success in consulting is about leveraging your unique strengths, not about adhering to myths or stereotypes.

REFLECTION

Addressing common myths about consulting can help clarify whether it is a good fit for you.

1. *What myths about consulting surprised you the most, and why?*
2. *How did debunking these myths affect your perception of consulting as a viable career option?*
3. *Are there any personal myths or assumptions you hold about consulting that need re-evaluation?*

EXERCISE: DEBUNK YOUR PERSONAL MYTHS

Identify any personal myths or misconceptions about consulting and challenge them with evidence from what you have learned.

Step 1: Write down any personal myths or assumptions you have about consulting.

Step 2: For each myth, list at least one piece of evidence or insight from the chapters that challenges or debunks it.

Step 3: Reflect on how re-evaluating these myths impacts your perception of consulting as a career option.

4: TYPES OF CONSULTING ROLES FOR TECHNICAL EXPERTS

As a technical professional considering solo consulting, understanding the variety of consulting roles available is a key step in your decision-making process.

Consulting is not a one-size-fits-all career; it encompasses a broad spectrum of opportunities that can align with unique skills, interests, and career goals.

This chapter will explore the various consulting roles suitable for technical experts, the niche specialisations that can set you apart, and the clients and projects you might encounter.

This exploration will help you identify potential paths within consulting that match your strengths and preferences.

4.1 FREELANCE CONSULTING: PROJECT-BASED EXPERTISE

Freelance consulting is one of the most common entry points into the consulting world, particularly for technical professionals. In this model, you are hired on a project basis to provide specific expertise, whether designing a software solution, conducting data analysis, or developing engineering prototypes.

Freelance consultants often work with small to medium-sized businesses, startups, or even larger companies that require specialised skills for short-term projects.

Key Characteristics of Freelance Consulting:

- **Project-Based Work:** Freelance consultants typically work on defined projects with clear start and end points. Engagements can last from a few weeks to several months, depending on the project scope.
- **Flexibility:** Freelancers have the flexibility to choose which projects to undertake, allowing them to focus on work that aligns with their skills and interests.
- **Diverse Clients:** Freelance consultants often work with a wide variety of clients across different industries, gaining exposure to diverse challenges and solutions.
- **Independence:** As a freelancer, you operate independently, managing your workload, setting your rates, and handling client interactions on your own terms.

Freelance consulting is ideal for those who enjoy hands-on problem-solving and prefer a steady flow of varied projects. It offers the opportunity to build a diverse portfolio and rapidly gain experience across different sectors.

> **AI Reflection Prompt:** *How can I determine if freelance consulting suits my skills and career goals?*

4.2 CONTRACT CONSULTING: LONGER-TERM ENGAGEMENTS

Contract consulting involves longer-term engagements, where you may work with a client for several months or even years.

These roles are often more integrated with the client's operations, resembling traditional employment but without the long-term commitment.

Depending on the nature of the project and client preferences, contract consultants might work on-site alongside the client's team or remotely.

Key Characteristics of Contract Consulting:

- **Extended Engagements:** Contracts typically last from six months to a few years, providing a more stable and predictable income stream than short-term freelance projects.
- **Team Integration:** Contract consultants often work closely with client teams, contributing their expertise as if they were part of the organisation, which can offer a deeper, more sustained impact.
- **Specialised Roles:** Many contract consultants are brought in for highly specialised tasks that require ongoing attention, such as managing a complex IT transition, leading a critical engineering project, or providing sustained technical support.

Contract consulting is well suited for those who prefer more stability and the opportunity to immerse themselves in a client's environment.

It combines the benefits of consulting with the familiarity of longer-term projects, making it a good fit for those who enjoy building lasting relationships and seeing the long-term results of their work.

> **AI Reflection Prompt:** *What are the benefits and challenges of contract consulting compared to other models?*

4.3 ADVISORY CONSULTING: PROVIDING STRATEGIC GUIDANCE

Advisory consulting focuses on providing strategic advice and guidance rather than direct implementation. This role is typically reserved for more experienced consultants who have a deep understanding of their field and can offer insights that influence high-level decision-making. Advisory consultants might work with executive teams, boards, or senior management to help shape the direction of projects, initiatives, or entire organisations.

Key Characteristics of Advisory Consulting:

- **High-Level Engagement:** Advisory roles involve working with decision-makers to provide strategic insights, identify opportunities, and mitigate risks. The focus is on shaping strategy rather than executing tasks.
- **Expertise-Driven:** Advisory consultants are valued for their depth of knowledge and experience. They are seen as thought leaders who can provide unique perspectives that clients cannot easily find internally.
- **Flexible Structure:** Advisory consulting often involves flexible arrangements, such as retainer agreements or periodic consulting sessions, which allow clients to access your expertise as needed.

Advisory consulting is ideal for seasoned professionals who have accumulated significant experience and are looking to leverage that knowledge in a strategic capacity.

It offers the chance to influence high-stakes decisions and contribute to the broader direction of organisations without getting bogged down in day-to-day operations.

> **AI Reflection Prompt:** *What expertise or experience do I need to transition into advisory consulting?*

4.4 TECHNICAL SPECIALIST CONSULTING: DEEP NICHE EXPERTISE

Technical specialist consulting involves offering highly specialised services within a specific niche.

This role is perfect for experts who have a deep understanding of a particular technology, methodology, or industry practice.

Clients seeking technical specialist consultants often look for someone who can provide solutions beyond standard knowledge, tapping into cutting-edge developments or highly technical fields.

Key Characteristics of Technical Specialist Consulting:

- **Deep Niche Focus:** These consultants are hired for their expert knowledge in very specific areas, such as cybersecurity, AI algorithms, biomedical engineering, or advanced data analytics.
- **Problem-Solving at the Frontier:** Technical specialists often tackle the most challenging problems, providing insights that generalist consultants do not readily offer.
- **High Demand and Premium Rates:** Due to the depth of their expertise, technical specialists can command higher rates, especially if their skills are rare and highly sought after.

Technical specialist consulting is best suited for those who are passionate about a specific area and enjoy delving deep into complex, specialised challenges.

It offers the opportunity to be recognised as a leading expert in your field and work on projects that push the boundaries of current knowledge and practice.

> **AI Reflection Prompt:** *How can I identify a niche where my technical expertise would be in high demand?*

4.5 MANAGEMENT CONSULTING: BRIDGING TECHNICAL AND BUSINESS STRATEGY

Management consulting for technical professionals involves bridging the gap between technical expertise and business strategy.

These consultants help organisations improve efficiency, optimise processes, and adopt new technologies to align with their overall business goals.

Management consultants often work with transforming companies, aiding them in navigating change and achieving strategic objectives.

Key Characteristics of Management Consulting:

- **Cross-Functional Expertise:** Management consultants need to understand both the technical and business aspects of an organisation. This requires a broad skill set that includes technical knowledge, strategic thinking, and change management.
- **Impactful Projects:** These roles often involve high-impact projects such as process optimisation, technology integration, or operational transformation, making them ideal for those who want to drive significant change.
- **Client-Focused:** Management consultants work closely with client stakeholders, necessitating strong communication skills and the ability to translate technical concepts into business terms.

Management consulting is a good fit for technical professionals interested in business strategy who want to play a key role in helping organisations succeed.

It offers the opportunity to apply technical skills in a broader context and to contribute to companies' strategic direction.

> **AI Reflection Prompt:** *How can I leverage my technical knowledge to bridge the gap between technical expertise and business strategy in management consulting?*

4.6 FINDING YOUR FIT: CHOOSING THE RIGHT CONSULTING ROLE

With many consulting roles available, finding the right fit depends on your skills, interests, and career goals.

- **Evaluate Your Strengths and Interests:** Reflect on which aspects of your current role you enjoy the most. Do you thrive on hands-on technical work, or are you drawn to strategy and big-picture thinking? Understanding your preferences will help you identify the consulting role that best suits you.
- **Consider Your Desired Level of Client Interaction:** Some roles, such as advisory or management consulting, involve

significant client interaction and relationship-building. If you prefer independent work, technical specialist or freelance consulting might be a better fit.

- **Assess Your Risk Tolerance and Financial Goals:** Freelance and contract consulting offer flexibility but also come with income variability. If financial stability is a priority, you may prefer longer-term contract roles or building a steady base of advisory clients.
- **Think About Your Desired Impact:** Do you want to solve immediate technical problems, influence strategic decisions, or drive large-scale change? Different consulting roles offer varying levels of impact, so consider where you can make the most meaningful contribution.

The world of consulting offers a diverse range of roles for technical professionals, each with its own set of opportunities and challenges.

Whether you are drawn to the project variety of freelance consulting, the strategic influence of advisory roles, or the deep expertise of technical specialist consulting, there is likely a consulting path that aligns with your skills and aspirations.

Understanding the different consulting roles available can help you identify where you might best fit and how your unique strengths can be leveraged to provide value to clients.

As you continue exploring the possibility of a consulting career, consider how these roles resonate with your professional goals and personal preferences. Consulting is a versatile field; finding the right niche can make all the difference in your success and satisfaction as a consultant.

AI Reflection Prompt: *How can I evaluate whether I prefer consulting roles with high client interaction, like advisory or management consulting, or more independent roles, like freelance or technical specialist consulting?*

KEY CONCEPTS

The consulting landscape offers diverse roles tailored to the skills and aspirations of technical professionals. Understanding the differences between freelance, contract, advisory, technical specialist, and management consulting helps identify where your strengths and preferences align. Choosing the right niche ensures meaningful work, career satisfaction, and success as a solo consultant.

4.1 Freelance Consulting: Project-Based Expertise

Ideal for those who enjoy varied, hands-on problem-solving and want to build a diverse portfolio quickly.

Project-Based Work: Defined projects with clear start and end points.

Flexibility: Freedom to choose projects that align with personal skills and interests.

Diverse Clients: Exposure to a variety of industries and challenges.

Independence: Freelancers manage their workload, rates, and client interactions independently.

4.2 Contract Consulting: Longer-Term Engagements

Suitable for those seeking stability, long-term relationships, and deeper immersion in client environments.

Extended Engagements: Typically last several months to years, offering stable income.

Team Integration: Embedded within client teams, contributing as if part of the organisation.

Specialised Roles: Often hired for ongoing, high-priority tasks like engineering projects.

4.3 Advisory Consulting: Providing Strategic Guidance

Ideal for seasoned professionals interested in leveraging their expertise to guide big-picture decisions without daily execution.

High-Level Engagement: Works with decision-makers to influence strategy and mitigate risks.

Expertise-Driven: Relies on deep knowledge and experience.

Flexible Structure: Often involves retainers or periodic consultations.

4.4 Technical Specialist Consulting: Deep Niche Expertise

Perfect for experts passionate about niche areas and tackling highly technical challenges.

Deep Niche Focus: Centres on expertise in highly specialised fields like AI, cybersecurity, or advanced engineering.

Problem Solving at the Frontier: Addresses complex, cutting-edge challenges.

High Demand and Premium Rates: Skills scarcity can command top compensation.

4.5 Management Consulting: Bridging Technical and Business Strategy

Best for professionals who want to drive organisational change and align technical efforts with business goals.

Cross-Functional Expertise: Combines technical knowledge with strategic thinking and change management.

Impactful Projects: Focuses on large-scale transformations like process optimisation or technology integration.

Client-Focused: Involves translating technical concepts into business terms for stakeholders.

4.6 Finding Your Fit: Choosing the Right Consulting Role

Evaluate Strengths and Interests: Identify whether you prefer technical problem-solving or strategic planning.

Consider Client Interaction: Assess your comfort level with high client engagement versus independent work.

Assess Risk Tolerance and Financial Goals: Freelance roles offer flexibility but income variability; contract roles provide more stability.

Determine Desired Impact: Decide whether you wish to focus on immediate problem-solving, strategic influence, or transformational change.

REFLECTION

1. *Which types of consulting roles discussed in this chapter do you find most intriguing? Why?*
2. *How do your current skills and expertise align with the consulting roles that interest you?*
3. *Are there any roles you had not considered before that might be a good fit for your background?*

EXERCISE: COMPARE AND CONTRAST: CONSULTING VS. YOUR CURRENT ROLE

Create a comparison chart to visualise the differences between consulting and your current role or career path.

Step 1: Draw a three-column chart. Label the columns "Current Role," "Consulting," and "Insights."

Step 2: List key factors such as job security, income potential, work-life balance, skill utilisation, and personal fulfilment in the rows.

Step 3: Fill in the characteristics of your current role and consulting for each factor.

Step 4: Reflect on the insights column. What do you notice about the differences and similarities? How do they influence your thinking about a potential transition to consulting?

5: CONSULTING VS. TRADITIONAL EMPLOYMENT

Deciding whether to pursue solo consulting or remain in traditional employment significantly impacts your career trajectory, financial stability, work-life balance, and overall satisfaction.

Each path offers distinct advantages and challenges, and the right choice depends on your personal goals, values, and risk tolerance.

This chapter will compare consulting with traditional employment across several key factors, including job security, benefits, professional growth, and alignment with career aspirations. By understanding these differences, you can make a more informed decision about which path best suits your needs.

5.1 JOB SECURITY AND FINANCIAL STABILITY

One of the most notable differences between consulting and traditional employment is their level of job security and financial stability.

Traditional Employment: Steady Paycheck and Stability

Traditional employment provides the predictability of a steady paycheck, benefits, and a sense of job security. For many, this financial stability is a major draw, offering peace of mind and the ability to plan for the future with a consistent income stream.

Traditional jobs often include benefits such as health insurance, retirement contributions, paid time off, and other perks that add significant value in addition to salary.

Employers in traditional roles also bear the risks of market fluctuations, downturns, and business uncertainties. This provides a buffer for employees who continue to receive their paychecks regardless of the company's immediate challenges.

This security particularly appeals to those with dependents, financial obligations, or a preference for a more predictable lifestyle.

Consulting: Variable Income and Entrepreneurial Risk

In contrast, consulting comes with income variability and the absence of traditional benefits. Consultants are paid per project or hourly, and there can be gaps between contracts when no income is generated.

This variability requires consultants to be financially savvy. They must set aside savings during peak periods to cover lean times and actively manage cash flow to maintain financial stability.

While consulting offers the potential for higher earnings, especially in high-demand niches, it also involves entrepreneurial risk.

As a consultant, you are responsible for generating your work, which can be both empowering and daunting. The security of consulting lies in your ability to build and maintain a strong client pipeline, adapt to changing market demands, and manage the financial uncertainties that come with self-employment.

> **AI Reflection Prompt:** *How can I evaluate whether I am comfortable transitioning from the steady income of traditional employment to the financial variability of consulting?*

5.2 BENEFITS AND PERKS

Traditional Employment: Comprehensive Benefits Packages

One of the significant advantages of traditional employment is the comprehensive benefits package that often accompanies a full-time role. These benefits typically include health insurance, retirement plans, life insurance, disability coverage, paid vacation and sick leave, and access to professional development resources.

These perks provide a safety net that enhances overall compensation and contributes to a more secure and stable lifestyle.

For many employees, benefits play a critical role in their financial and personal well-being, reducing the burden of out-of-pocket expenses for healthcare and retirement savings. The convenience of having these benefits managed by the employer is a significant draw for those who prefer not to handle these details independently.

Consulting: Customisable but Self-Managed Benefits

As a consultant, you are responsible for securing your own benefits, which can be both challenging and rewarding. While consultants must pay for health insurance, retirement contributions, and other benefits out of pocket, they also have the flexibility to tailor these choices to their specific needs.

For example, consultants can choose high-deductible health plans that align with their risk tolerance, select retirement investment strategies that match their financial goals, and opt for benefits most relevant to their circumstances.

The downside is that managing and funding these benefits requires additional effort, and costs can be significantly higher without the purchasing power of a large employer.

Consultants must also consider the lack of paid time off, which means that any time away from work directly impacts income. Traditional employment may offer a more appealing package for those prioritising comprehensive benefits and the convenience of employer-provided perks.

AI Reflection Prompt: *What steps should I take to replace the benefits I currently receive in traditional employment as a consultant?*

5.3 PROFESSIONAL GROWTH AND CAREER DEVELOPMENT

Traditional Employment: Structured Growth Paths

In traditional employment, structured career paths, mentorship opportunities, training programs, and regular performance reviews often support professional growth.

Many companies invest in their employees' development, offering clear promotion tracks, tuition reimbursement for further education, and opportunities to take on leadership roles or cross-functional projects.

This structure provides a clear roadmap for advancing within an organisation, with defined milestones and expectations.

Traditional employment offers a supportive environment for professionals who value a clear sense of progression and the security of a guided development path.

The predictability of titles, roles, and career ladders can be reassuring, while the collaborative nature of traditional workplaces often fosters learning and networking opportunities that are integral to professional growth.

Consulting: Self-Directed Learning and Diverse Experiences

Consulting, on the other hand, offers a more self-directed approach to professional growth.

Consultants are responsible for identifying and pursuing their own learning opportunities, including certifications, online courses, industry conferences, or acquiring new skills through diverse client projects.

The variety of consulting work often accelerates learning, as consultants are exposed to different challenges, industries, and technologies that broaden their expertise.

While consulting lacks the structured growth paths of traditional employment, it compensates for this with the freedom to shape your career trajectory.

As they gain experience, consultants can pivot to new niches, scale their services, or even transition into advisory roles. Consulting offers a dynamic and flexible career path for those who thrive on independence and are motivated by the prospect of creating growth opportunities.

> **AI Reflection Prompt:** *How does consulting offer opportunities for growth compared to traditional employment, and how can I align these opportunities with my long-term career goals?*

5.4 WORK-LIFE BALANCE AND FLEXIBILITY

Traditional Employment: Predictable Routine with Limitations

Traditional employment typically offers a more predictable work schedule, with set hours and a defined work environment. This structure can provide a routine conducive to work-life balance, especially when combined with certain benefits from companies, such as paid time off, parental leave, and flexible work policies.

However, traditional roles also come with limitations, such as fixed office hours, commuting requirements, and the need to align with company policies and goals.

Traditional employment can be a good fit for those seeking a stable routine and the ability to disconnect from work after hours. However, the rigidity of traditional roles can also be a drawback for individuals who crave more autonomy over their time and work environment.

Consulting: Flexibility with Boundaries

One of the hallmark advantages of consulting is its flexibility.

Consultants can often set their hours, choose their work location, and have greater control over their workload.

This flexibility allows consultants to balance personal and professional responsibilities better, pursue other interests, or even travel while working remotely. However, this flexibility requires strong boundaries. Without the structure of a traditional job, work can easily spill into personal time, leading to long hours and potential burnout.

Successful consultants can establish clear boundaries, manage their time effectively, and resist the temptation to overcommit.

For those who value autonomy and the ability to shape their work-life balance, consulting offers a level of control that traditional roles often lack.

> **AI Reflection Prompt:** *How can I take advantage of the flexibility consulting offers while maintaining a healthy work-life balance?*

5.5 ALIGNMENT WITH CAREER GOALS AND PERSONAL VALUES

Ultimately, the choice between consulting and traditional employment hinges on how each path aligns with your career goals and personal values.

Traditional Employment: Stability and Long-Term Commitment

Traditional employment is well suited to individuals who prioritise stability, clear career progression, and the benefits of working within a structured organisation.

It offers a supportive environment for those who prefer steady work, defined roles, and the security of a long-term commitment. For many, belonging to a team and contributing to a larger organisational mission are key drivers of job satisfaction.

Consulting: Autonomy and Entrepreneurial Spirit

Consulting appeals to those who value autonomy, variety, and the entrepreneurial challenge of building their own business.

It aligns with professionals who wish to follow their own path, solve diverse problems, and directly impact client outcomes.

Consulting also offers the opportunity to align work with personal passions and values, allowing individuals to choose projects that resonate with them and avoid those that do not.

Consulting provides a unique and fulfilling alternative to traditional employment for technical professionals who are comfortable with risk, enjoy continuous learning, and are motivated by the prospect of steering their own careers.

The choice between consulting and traditional employment is deeply personal and depends on individual priorities, risk tolerance, and career aspirations. Both paths offer unique benefits and challenges, and neither is inherently better.

You can determine which option best suits your needs by carefully considering factors such as job security, benefits, professional growth, work-life balance, and alignment with your goals.

Whether you choose the stability of traditional employment or the independence of consulting, the most important factor is that your choice reflects your values and supports your vision for your professional future.

Consulting is not a one-size-fits-all solution, but for those ready to embrace its challenges and rewards, it can be a highly satisfying and impactful career path.

AI Reflection Prompts. *What steps can I take to expand my skills for consulting?*

How can I assess whether consulting or traditional employment better aligns with my personal values and professional aspirations?

KEY CONCEPTS

The choice between consulting and traditional employment depends on personal priorities, career aspirations, and risk tolerance. While traditional employment offers stability and structured growth, consulting provides autonomy, variety, and entrepreneurial opportunities. Both paths have unique benefits and challenges, and the best choice is one that aligns with your values and professional vision.

5.1 Job Security and Financial Stability

Traditional Employment:

Offers predictable income, benefits, and job security.

Employers buffer market risks, ensuring steady paychecks during downturns.

Appeals to those with dependents, financial obligations, or a preference for stability.

Consulting:

Income is variable and project-dependent, requiring financial planning and cash flow management.

Success relies on building a strong client pipeline and adapting to market demands.

Higher earnings are possible but come with entrepreneurial risks.

5.2 Benefits and Perks

Traditional Employment:

Provides comprehensive benefits like health insurance, retirement plans, and paid time off.

Employer-managed benefits reduce the burden on employees.

Consulting:

Requires self-management of benefits, offering flexibility to customise them to individual needs.

Benefits such as health insurance and retirement contributions can be more costly and time-consuming to arrange.

No paid time off; time away from work impacts income.

5.3 Professional Growth and Career Development

Traditional Employment:

Offers structured career paths with mentorship, training programs, and promotion opportunities.

Presentas a clear roadmap for advancement, with collaborative environments fostering learning and networking.

Consulting:

Facilitates self-directed growth through certifications, online courses, and diverse client projects.

Offers dynamic career trajectories with opportunities to pivot into new niches or advisory roles.

Ideal for those who value independence and accelerated learning.

5.4 Work-Life Balance and Flexibility

Traditional Employment:

Features predictable schedules and routines, with benefits like parental leave and paid vacations.

Limitations include fixed hours, commuting, and alignment with company policies.

Consulting:

Provides flexibility to set hours, choose work location, and balance responsibilities.

Requires strong boundaries to prevent overwork and burnout.

Appeals to those seeking autonomy in their work-life balance.

· · ·

5.5 Alignment with Career Goals and Personal Values

Traditional Employment:

Suits individuals prioritising stability, clear career progression, and team collaboration.

Offers a supportive environment with a long-term commitment to organisational goals.

Consulting:

Aligns with professionals who value autonomy, variety, and entrepreneurial challenges.

Allows the selection of projects that resonate with personal values and avoids undesirable ones.

Encourages independence and has a direct impact on client outcomes.

5.6 Weighing the Options

Traditional Employment:

Best for those who prefer security, defined roles, and organisational support.

It provides a steady path for financial stability and structured growth.

Consulting:

Ideal for individuals who are comfortable with risk and motivated by independence.

While it requires resilience, adaptability, and self-management, it offers significant rewards.

REFLECTION

Comparing consulting to traditional employment can help clarify whether a transition makes sense for you.

1. *What are the main differences between consulting and traditional employment that stand out to you?*
2. *Reflect on your current or past job experiences—what elements would you like to keep or change in a consulting role?*
3. *How do the pros and cons of consulting compare to your current employment situation in terms of career goals, lifestyle, and satisfaction?*

EXERCISE: COMPARE YOUR IDEAL WORK SCENARIO

Step 1: Identify Key Work Factors

Step 2: Rate Each Factor for Traditional Employment

Step 3: Rate Each Factor for Consulting

Step 4: Compare and Reflect

Step 5: Identify Your Priorities

Step 6: Summarise Your Insights.

PART 2: SELF-ASSESSMENT: ARE YOU READY FOR CONSULTING?

The question isn't who is going to let me; it's who is going to stop me.

AYN RAND

6: PERSONAL AND PROFESSIONAL READINESS

Transitioning to solo consulting is a significant decision that extends beyond professional considerations; it touches on your personality, career aspirations, and lifestyle preferences.

Consulting is not just a job—it is a way of working and living that requires a particular set of skills, attitudes, and motivations.

In this chapter, we will introduce a detailed self-assessment tool designed to help you evaluate whether consulting is a good fit for you personally and professionally. By reflecting on these questions, you can gain clarity on your readiness for the consulting path.

6.1 THE IMPORTANCE OF SELF-ASSESSMENT

Before entering the world of consulting, it is crucial to take a step back and honestly assess whether this path aligns with your values and career goals.

Self-assessment is not about judging your abilities or aspirations but rather about gaining a clear understanding of where your strengths lie and where you might need to develop or adapt.

It is about ensuring that the decision to consult is driven by informed self-awareness rather than external pressures or misconceptions. Consulting can offer tremendous rewards, but it also demands resilience, adaptability, and a proactive approach to career management.

The following self-assessment is divided into three key areas: personality fit, career goals alignment, and lifestyle considerations. Use these questions to guide your reflection and identify areas where you feel confident, as well as those that may require further thought or preparation.

> **AI Reflection Prompt:** *How can I assess whether consulting aligns with my skills, personality, and career aspirations? What specific factors should I consider?*

6.2 PERSONALITY FIT: ARE YOU SUITED TO CONSULTING?

Consulting requires a blend of independence, self-motivation, and the ability to navigate uncertainty. Reflect on the following questions to assess whether your personality aligns with these demands:

1. **Do you thrive on independence and autonomy?** Consulting is well-suited for individuals who enjoy working independently and making their own decisions. If you find fulfilment in taking charge of your work, setting your own schedule, and driving projects without needing constant guidance, consulting could be a good fit for you. Conversely, if you prefer the structure and support of a team environment, you may need to consider how you will compensate for the absence of these elements in consulting.

2. **Are you comfortable with risk and uncertainty?** Consulting involves a level of risk not present in traditional employment, including income variability and the need to find new clients continually. Assess your comfort with these uncertainties. Are you adaptable and resourceful when faced with unexpected

challenges? Do you view risks as opportunities for growth, or do they cause significant stress?

3. **How do you handle rejection and setbacks?** In consulting, not every pitch will be successful, and not every client relationship will go smoothly. Your ability to handle rejection, learn from setbacks, and keep moving forward is critical to success in this field. Reflect on how you typically respond to challenges—do you bounce back quickly, or do setbacks tend to derail your motivation?

4. **Do you enjoy problem-solving and continuous learning?** Consulting is fundamentally about solving problems and providing value through your expertise. As industries and technologies evolve rapidly, a commitment to continuous learning is essential. Consulting can be a highly satisfying career if you are naturally curious, enjoy tackling new challenges, and are committed to ongoing professional development.

5. **Can you manage your time and stay self-disciplined?** Without the structure of a traditional job, consultants must create their own routines and manage their time effectively. Consider your ability to set goals, prioritise tasks, and maintain productivity without external oversight. Are you disciplined in your approach to work, or do you struggle with procrastination or time management?

AI Reflection Prompt: *What steps can I take to address potential gaps regarding whether I am suited to the independence and self-motivation required for consulting?*

6.3 CAREER GOALS ALIGNMENT: DOES CONSULTING SUPPORT YOUR PROFESSIONAL ASPIRATIONS?

To determine if consulting aligns with your career goals, reflect on what you want to achieve professionally.

Consulting can provide unique opportunities for growth, but it is essential to ensure these opportunities align with your long-term vision.

1. **What are your primary career goals?** Start by identifying your top career goals. Are you seeking financial independence, a flexible work-life balance, the opportunity to work on diverse projects, or the ability to influence decisions at a strategic level? Understanding your core motivations will help you determine if consulting is a pathway that supports your aspirations.

2. **Do you value variety or specialisation in your work?** Consulting offers the chance to work across various projects and industries, which can be exciting for those who thrive on diversity and continuous learning. However, if you prefer deep specialisation and a consistent focus on a specific type of work, consider how consulting can fit into this preference. There are consulting roles that cater to both breadth and depth, but clarity on your preference will guide your niche selection.

3. **How important is career stability to you?** If career stability and a predictable trajectory are critical to your satisfaction, consulting may present challenges. Consulting offers the potential for growth and independence but lacks the clear, structured progression found in traditional employment. Reflect on your tolerance for career ambiguity and your willingness to navigate a less-defined path.

4. **Do you aspire to leadership and influence?** Consulting provides opportunities to advise clients, influence strategic decisions, and position yourself as a thought leader in your field. If these aspects resonate with your goals, consulting can offer a platform to achieve them. However, consider whether you are comfortable with the indirect nature of leadership in consulting, where you may influence outcomes without formal authority.

5. **Are you prepared to take on a business owner's mindset?** Consulting is not just about delivering expertise; it's also about running a business. This includes marketing your services, managing finances, and continually seeking new opportunities.

Assess whether you are prepared to embrace this entrepreneurial aspect of consulting, as it plays a significant role in your long-term success.

AI Reflection Prompt: *How can I evaluate my comfort level with the financial and professional risks associated with consulting?*

6.4 LIFESTYLE CONSIDERATIONS: DOES CONSULTING FIT YOUR DESIRED WAY OF LIVING?

Consulting impacts not only your professional life but also your lifestyle. Considering how consulting aligns with your personal needs, family commitments, and overall well-being is important.

1. **How important is work-life balance to you?** Consulting can offer flexibility but also requires strong boundaries to prevent work from overtaking personal time. Reflect on how consulting might impact your work-life balance. Are you disciplined enough to manage your schedule, or do you struggle to disconnect from work? Understanding your need for balance will help you assess how consulting fits your lifestyle.

2. **Do you have a strong support system?** Consulting can sometimes be isolating, especially if you're used to working in team settings. Consider whether you have a robust personal or professional support system to provide encouragement, feedback, and connection. This could include family, mentors, or a network of fellow consultants.

3. **Are you prepared for the potential financial implications?** Consulting involves managing your finances, including health insurance, retirement savings, and handling periods of variable income. Assess your financial readiness and whether you have the resources or willingness to manage these aspects independently. Are you comfortable budgeting and planning for lean periods, or do you rely heavily on the financial stability of a traditional job?

4. **How do you feel about travel and remote work?** Depending on your niche, consulting may involve travel or remote work. Consider how this aligns with your personal preferences. Do you enjoy the flexibility of working from anywhere, or do you prefer the routine of a dedicated workspace? Are you open to travelling for client engagements, or do your commitments keep you closer to home?

5. **What are your non-negotiables?** Finally, identify your non-negotiables—those aspects of your lifestyle or work with which you are unwilling to compromise. This could include spending time with family, pursuing hobbies, or maintaining a specific work environment. Ensuring that consulting can accommodate these non-negotiables will help you make a decision that aligns with your values and priorities.

AI Reflection Prompt: *How can I assess whether consulting aligns with my long-term career goals and supports my professional aspirations?*

6.5 REFLECTING ON YOUR READINESS

After considering the questions in this self-assessment, take some time to reflect on your answers. Look for patterns that indicate whether consulting aligns with your personality, career goals, and lifestyle preferences.

If consulting resonates with many of your priorities but reveals areas of concern, consider how you might address these challenges. Further learning, strategic planning, or seeking mentorship could help bridge the gaps.

It's also important to acknowledge that no career path is perfect. Every option comes with trade-offs, and the goal of this self-assessment is not to find a flawless fit but to clarify whether consulting is a viable and fulfilling path for you.

Determining your readiness for consulting is a deeply personal process that requires honest reflection on your personality, professional aspirations, and lifestyle needs.

By engaging with this self-assessment, you have taken a crucial step in understanding whether consulting aligns with your unique strengths and goals. Use these insights as a foundation for your decision-making, and continue to explore how consulting fits into your vision for your career and life.

As you move forward, remember that readiness for consulting is not about having all the answers but about embracing the journey with a clear understanding of its responsibilities.

Whether you decide consulting is right for you now or in the future, this self-assessment is a valuable tool for guiding your career choices.

> **AI Reflection Prompt:** *What are three specific actions I can take to evaluate and improve my readiness for a consulting career?*

KEY CONCEPTS

Use the self-assessment tool to evaluate whether consulting aligns with your personality, career goals, and lifestyle preferences. This honest reflection helps identify strengths to leverage and challenges to address, ensuring a more informed and fulfilling career decision. Readiness for consulting is less about perfection and more about embracing the journey with clarity and purpose.

6.1 The Importance of Self-Assessment

Self-assessment helps clarify whether consulting aligns with your values, strengths, and career aspirations.

It identifies areas where you are well suited for consulting and highlights potential gaps to address.

Consulting requires resilience, adaptability, and a proactive approach —qualities essential for success.

6.2 Personality Fit: Are You Suited to Consulting?

Independence: Thrives on autonomy, decision-making, and self-direction.

Comfort with Risk: Adapts to income variability and uncertainty in securing clients.

Resilience: Bounces back from rejection and setbacks with motivation intact.

Problem-Solving: Enjoys tackling challenges and is committed to continuous learning.

Self-Discipline: Effectively manages time, sets goals, and maintains productivity without external oversight.

6.3 Career Goals Alignment: Does Consulting Support Your Aspirations?

Primary Goals: Aligns with ambitions such as financial independence, flexibility, or strategic influence.

Variety or Specialisation: Matches your preference for diverse experiences or deep expertise.

Stability: Balances a tolerance for ambiguity with opportunities for growth and independence.

Leadership and Influence: Positions you to advise, influence, and establish thought leadership.

Entrepreneurial Mindset: Combines expertise delivery with business management responsibilities.

6.4 Lifestyle Considerations: Does Consulting Fit Your Way of Living?

Work-Life Balance: Offers flexibility but requires boundaries to avoid burnout.

Support System: Leverages personal and professional networks for encouragement and connection.

Financial Readiness: Manages independent finances, including insurance, retirement savings, and lean periods.

Travel and Remote Work: Aligns with preferences for mobility or location stability.

Non-Negotiables: Ensures consulting accommodates essential personal or professional priorities.

6.5 Reflecting on Your Readiness

Look for patterns in your self-assessment to determine if consulting aligns with your priorities and strengths.

Address identified challenges through learning, mentorship, or strategic planning.

Acknowledge trade-offs; no career path is perfect, but consulting should support your values and vision.

REFLECTION

How do your personal values, goals, and lifestyle align with the realities of consulting? What aspects of your current professional life are you most eager to change or maintain through consulting?

EXERCISE: SELF-ASSESSMENT CHECKLIST FOR READINESS

Step 1: Create a Readiness Checklist. Develop a checklist that covers key areas of personal and professional readiness for consulting. Include factors such as:

- Motivation for consulting
- Alignment with personal values
- Willingness to take risks
- Time management skills
- Support system (family, friends, mentors)
- Financial stability and preparedness
- Desire for independence and control over work
- Flexibility and adaptability
- Comfort with uncertainty and change

Step 2: Rate Your Readiness. Rate each factor on a scale of 1 to 5, where 1 indicates not ready and 5 indicates fully ready. Be honest with yourself about your current position in each area.

Step 3: Identify Strengths and Areas for Improvement. Review your ratings and identify your strengths—areas where you feel fully ready for consulting. Also, note areas where your readiness is lower, and consider what actions you could take to enhance your preparedness.

Step 4: Reflect on Your Results. Summarise your findings in a brief reflection. What are your key takeaways from this self-assessment? How does your overall readiness align with your decision to pursue consulting?

7: EVALUATING YOUR SKILL SET FOR CONSULTING

E mbarking on a consulting career requires a broad range of skills beyond your core technical expertise.

While your specialised knowledge is the cornerstone of your consulting value, success in this field also depends on your ability to communicate effectively, manage client relationships, and handle the business aspects of running a consulting practice.

This chapter will guide you in evaluating your skill set across three key areas: technical expertise, communication skills, and business knowledge. By identifying your strengths and areas for improvement, you can better prepare for the demands of consulting and position yourself as a valuable asset to potential clients.

7.1 ASSESSING YOUR TECHNICAL EXPERTISE

Your technical skills are the primary reason clients hire you as a consultant. These skills form the foundation of the services you offer and the solutions you provide. It is important to have a clear understanding of your technical strengths, the areas where you excel, and how these align with market demand.

Key Questions to Evaluate Your Technical Expertise:

1. **What are your core technical skills?** Begin by listing your core technical skills—the specific areas where you have deep knowledge and experience. Are you an expert in a particular programming language, engineering process, scientific methodology, or data analysis technique? Clearly defining your core competencies will help you identify your unique value proposition as a consultant.

2. **How current and relevant are your skills?** The consulting landscape is dynamic, with client needs often driven by emerging trends and technologies. Evaluate whether your skills are up to date and relevant to current market demands. Are you proficient in the latest tools, software, or methodologies in your field? Consider investing in continuous learning to keep your expertise sharp and aligned with industry developments.

3. **Can you solve specific problems or offer specialised solutions?** Clients hire consultants to address specific challenges. Reflect on the problems you are best equipped to solve. Are there particular issues or pain points that your skills directly address? Defining the problems you can solve will help you market your services more effectively and target the right clients.

4. **Do you have a track record of success?** Consulting clients often look for evidence of past success. Consider your professional achievements, projects, or case studies that demonstrate your expertise. Do you have quantifiable results or testimonials that showcase your impact? A strong track record builds credibility and serves as a persuasive tool when pitching your services.

5. **Are you adaptable and willing to expand your skill set?** Consulting frequently requires flexibility, as you may encounter client needs that extend beyond your current expertise. Assess your adaptability and openness to learning new skills. Are you willing to explore adjacent areas of your

field or acquire complementary skills that could broaden your service offerings?

Action Steps:

- **Identify Skills to Highlight:** Based on your evaluation, pinpoint the technical skills that set you apart and align with market demand. These should be prominently featured in your consulting pitch, website, or LinkedIn profile.
- **Commit to Continuous Learning:** Create a plan for ongoing education to keep your skills relevant. This could include online courses, certifications, attending conferences, or engaging with professional communities.

   AI Reflection Prompt: *How can I position my core technical skills as the foundation of my consulting value?*

7.2 EVALUATING YOUR COMMUNICATION SKILLS

Communication is a critical skill in consulting, as it impacts every aspect of your interactions with clients—from initial engagement and pitching your services to delivering reports and managing ongoing relationships. Effective communication builds trust, clarifies expectations, and ensures that the value you provide is fully recognised.

Key Questions to Evaluate Your Communication Skills:

1. **How well do you articulate complex ideas?** As a consultant, you often need to explain technical concepts to clients who may not share your expertise. Evaluate your ability to break down complex ideas into clear, concise, and relatable terms. Can you tailor your communication style to suit different audiences, from technical stakeholders to executive decision-makers?
2. **Are you an active listener?** Consulting is more than providing solutions; it also involves understanding client needs. Active listening is essential for accurately diagnosing problems and

aligning recommendations with client expectations. Reflect on your listening skills: Do you ask probing questions, seek clarification, and show empathy for the client's perspective?

3. **Can you write effectively and professionally?** Written communication is a significant part of consulting, encompassing proposals, reports, emails, and presentations. Assess your writing skills in terms of clarity, structure, and professionalism. Are you able to convey your findings and recommendations in a way that is both informative and persuasive?

4. **How do you handle difficult conversations?** Consulting can involve navigating challenging situations, such as managing client expectations, addressing scope changes, or delivering bad news. Consider your comfort level with difficult conversations and your ability to remain calm, constructive, and solution-focused in these scenarios.

5. **Are you skilled at presenting and public speaking?** Presentations are a common aspect of consulting, whether you're pitching to potential clients, leading workshops, or sharing project outcomes. Evaluate your presentation skills, including your ability to engage an audience, use visual aids effectively, and handle Q&A sessions confidently.

Action Steps:

- **Practice and Refine Your Communication Skills:** Look for opportunities to enhance your communication skills, such as joining a public speaking group, seeking peer feedback, or engaging in role-play scenarios that simulate client interactions.
- **Develop a Communication Toolkit:** Create templates for proposals, reports, and presentations to customise for different clients. This will streamline your communication process and ensure consistency in conveying your message.

AI Reflection Prompt: *What steps can I take to align my technical skills with current market demands?*

7.3 ASSESSING YOUR BUSINESS KNOWLEDGE

Consulting is as much about business as it is about expertise. To run a successful consulting practice, you need a foundational understanding of business principles, including marketing, finance, and operations. Evaluating your business skills will help you identify areas needing additional knowledge or support.

Key Questions to Evaluate Your Business Knowledge:

1. **Do you understand the basics of marketing and sales?** Client acquisition is a key challenge in consulting, and effective marketing is essential for attracting and retaining clients. Assess your knowledge of marketing strategies, such as branding, networking, content creation, and digital marketing. Additionally, evaluate your sales skills—can you pitch your services convincingly, negotiate terms, and close deals?

2. **How comfortable are you with financial management?** As a consultant, you'll need to manage your finances, including budgeting, pricing, invoicing, and taxes. Reflect on your financial acumen—are you confident in setting your rates, forecasting income, and managing expenses? Do you understand the financial aspects of running a business, such as cash flow management and profitability analysis?

3. **Are you familiar with project management principles?** Effective project management ensures you deliver on time, within scope, and to the client's satisfaction. Evaluate your project management skills, including your ability to plan, organise, and track progress. Are you proficient with project management tools, such as Asana, Trello, or Microsoft Project, that can help you stay organised?

4. **Do you have experience with client relationship management?** Building and maintaining strong client relationships is crucial for long-term consulting success. Reflect

on your experience with client management—are you proactive in communication, responsive to client needs, and skilled at maintaining ongoing engagement? How do you handle client feedback, both positive and constructive?

5. **Can you set and achieve business goals?** Running a consulting business requires setting clear goals and working strategically to achieve them. Assess your goal-setting skills and your ability to develop action plans that drive results. Are you disciplined in tracking your progress and adjusting your approach when necessary?

Action Steps:

- **Strengthen Your Business Knowledge:** Consider taking courses or seeking mentorship in areas where your business knowledge may be lacking. This could include topics such as marketing, finance, or project management.
- **Utilise Business Tools:** Leverage tools and software that simplify business tasks, such as accounting software, CRM systems, or marketing platforms. These tools can help you manage your business more efficiently and save time for client-focused activities.

AI **Reflection Prompt:** *What business skills should I focus on developing to effectively run my consulting practice?*

7.4 IDENTIFYING STRENGTHS AND AREAS FOR IMPROVEMENT

After evaluating your technical, communication, and business skills, take stock of your overall readiness for consulting. Identify your key strengths—areas where you feel confident and capable—and consider how these strengths will serve you in your consulting practice. At the same time, acknowledge any gaps or areas for improvement.

Creating a personal development plan can help you address these gaps. This might include setting learning goals, seeking out training resources, or partnering with other consultants who complement your skills. Consulting is a journey; there is always room for growth and improvement. The key is to approach your development proactively and remain open to learning.

> **AI Reflection Prompt:** *What strategies can I use to build and maintain strong, long-term relationships with clients?*

7.5 LEVERAGING YOUR UNIQUE SKILL SET IN CONSULTING

Finally, consider how you can leverage your unique combination of skills in your consulting practice. Your technical expertise, communication abilities, and business knowledge contribute to your overall value proposition. Think about how these skills can differentiate you from other consultants and how you can use them to create a compelling narrative about the services you offer.

Consulting clients seek more than just technical solutions—they seek trusted advisors who can communicate effectively, manage projects smoothly, and deliver results that align with their business goals. By showcasing your well-rounded skill set, you position yourself as a consultant who offers expertise and the ability to drive meaningful impact.

> **AI Reflection Prompt:** *How can I create a plan for ongoing professional development to stay competitive and expand my consulting capabilities?*

Evaluating your skill set is crucial in preparing for a consulting career. By understanding your strengths and identifying areas for growth, you can build a foundation that supports your success as a consultant.

Whether you excel in technical expertise, communication, business knowledge, or all three, the key is to continually refine and expand your skills to meet the evolving demands of consulting.

Use this evaluation as a guide to focus your efforts, seek out learning opportunities, and develop the competencies that will set you apart in the consulting market.

With a clear understanding of your capabilities and a commitment to growth, you can confidently enter the consulting world and offer clients the full spectrum of your value.

KEY CONCEPTS

Evaluating and refining your skill set is essential for consulting success. By building on your technical expertise, honing communication skills, and strengthening business knowledge, you can confidently meet client demands and stand out in the consulting market. Use this chapter's framework to focus your efforts, address gaps, and develop a well-rounded foundation for your consulting career.

7.1 Assessing Your Technical Expertise

Identify your core technical skills and define your unique value proposition.

Ensure your skills are up to date and relevant to current market trends and client demands.

Focus on solving specific client problems and offering specialised solutions.

Build a strong track record of success through quantifiable results and testimonials.

Stay adaptable and open to expanding your expertise to meet diverse client needs.

7.2 Evaluating Your Communication Skills

Articulating Complex Ideas: Simplify technical concepts for diverse audiences, including non-technical stakeholders.

Active Listening: Understand client needs through empathy, probing questions, and seeking clarification.

Professional Writing: Develop clear, structured, and persuasive proposals, reports, and communications.

Handling Difficult Conversations: Manage client expectations, scope changes, and challenges constructively.

Presenting and Public Speaking: Deliver engaging presentations and confidently handle Q&A sessions.

7.3 Assessing Your Business Knowledge

Understand the basics of marketing and sales, including branding, networking, and client acquisition.

Develop financial management skills, such as budgeting, pricing, and cash flow tracking.

Apply project management principles to ensure timely and successful client deliverables.

Build and maintain strong client relationships through proactive communication and engagement.

Set clear business goals and work strategically to achieve them.

7.4 Identifying Strengths and Areas for Improvement

Reflect on your skill set to identify strengths that will benefit your consulting practice.

Acknowledge areas for growth and create a personal development plan with learning goals and training resources.

Partner with others or leverage tools to complement your skills and enhance efficiency.

7.5 Leveraging Your Unique Skill Set in Consulting

Combine technical expertise, communication abilities, and business knowledge to create a compelling value proposition.

Differentiate yourself by aligning your skills with client needs and showcasing your ability to deliver impactful results.

Position yourself as a trusted advisor by blending technical solutions with effective communication and project management.

REFLECTION

What are your strongest skills, and how do they align with the demands of consulting?

Are there specific skills you need to develop or refine to succeed in this field?

EXERCISE: SKILL GAP ANALYSIS

Step 1: List Your Core Skills. List your core skills, including technical expertise, soft skills, and any unique competencies that set you apart.

Step 2: Match Skills to Consulting Needs. Identify which skills are directly relevant to consulting and which are less applicable. Consider skills such as client communication, problem-solving, business acumen, and marketing.

Step 3: Identify Skill Gaps. Compare your current skills with those needed for consulting. Highlight any gaps where additional development may be required.

Step 4: Create a Skill Development Plan. For each skill gap identified, outline steps to develop or enhance these skills. This could include taking courses, seeking mentorship, practising through volunteer work, or gaining experience in your current role.

Step 5: Reflect on Your Plan. Write a brief reflection on your skill gap analysis. How prepared do you feel to bridge these gaps, and what are your next steps in building the skills necessary for consulting?

8: MINDSET AND MOTIVATION FOR CONSULTING

S uccess in consulting extends beyond technical skills and business acumen; it also hinges on having the right mindset. As a solo consultant, you are not just an expert in your field—you are also a business owner, a problem-solver, and an entrepreneur.

This multifaceted role demands a mindset that embraces adaptability, self-motivation, resilience, and a proactive approach to overcoming challenges.

In this chapter, we will explore the mindset needed for consulting and the motivations that can sustain you through the ups and downs of self-employment.

8.1 THE IMPORTANCE OF MINDSET IN CONSULTING

Mindset is a critical determinant of your success in consulting. While skills and knowledge are essential, your mindset shapes how you approach your work, respond to challenges, and interact with clients.

A positive, growth-oriented mindset can propel you forward, while a rigid or negative mindset can hold you back. Consulting requires a particular mental approach that is open to change, resilient to setbacks, and driven by a clear sense of purpose.

The mindset needed for consulting is not something you are born with; it is something you can cultivate and strengthen over time. By becoming aware of the key mental attributes contributing to consulting success, you can consciously develop these traits and better prepare yourself for the consulting journey.

> **AI Reflection Prompt:** *What mindset traits are most important for consulting success, and how can I develop them?*

8.2 ADAPTABILITY: THRIVING IN A CHANGING ENVIRONMENT

Adaptability is one of the most valuable traits for a consultant. The consulting landscape is constantly evolving, driven by changes in technology, market demands, and client expectations.

As a consultant, you will encounter a wide range of projects, industries, and client personalities. Adapting to new situations, learning quickly, and pivoting when necessary are crucial for maintaining relevance and delivering value.

Key Aspects of Adaptability in Consulting:

1. **Embracing Change:** In consulting, no two projects are exactly alike. You may work in different industries, apply new technologies, or address unfamiliar challenges. A willingness to embrace change and step outside your comfort zone is essential. Rather than viewing change as a disruption, see it as an opportunity to grow and expand your skill set.
2. **Learning Agility:** Adaptability is closely linked to your ability to quickly learn and apply new knowledge. This involves staying current with industry trends, continuously updating your skills, and being open to new ways of thinking. Consultants who are agile learners can provide innovative solutions and stay ahead of the competition.

3. **Navigating Uncertainty:** Consulting often involves dealing with ambiguity, whether it's unclear project scope, evolving client needs, or unpredictable market conditions. Cultivating a mindset that is comfortable with uncertainty allows you to remain calm and focused, even when the path forward is not immediately clear. Embrace uncertainty as a natural part of the consulting process and use it as a catalyst for creativity and problem-solving.

   AI Reflection Prompt: *How can I become more adaptable to thrive in the constantly changing environment of consulting?*

8.3 SELF-MOTIVATION: DRIVING YOUR OWN SUCCESS

Self-motivation is a cornerstone of consulting. Without the external structure and oversight provided by a traditional job, consultants must rely on their internal drive to set goals, stay on task, and overcome challenges.

The ability to motivate yourself—especially during slow periods or when facing setbacks—can make the difference between a thriving consulting practice and one that struggles to sustain momentum.

Key Aspects of Self-Motivation in Consulting:

1. **Setting Clear Goals:** Self-motivation starts with a clear vision of what you want to achieve. Set specific, measurable goals for your consulting business, such as landing a certain number of clients, achieving a revenue target, or developing a new service offering. Break these goals down into actionable steps and regularly review your progress to stay on track.
2. **Maintaining Discipline:** Consulting requires discipline in managing your time, following through on commitments, and consistently delivering high-quality work. Create routines that support your productivity, such as setting aside dedicated time for business development, client work, and professional growth. Discipline is about doing the work even when

motivation wanes, and it is crucial for sustaining long-term success.

3. **Finding Your "Why":** Understanding your deeper motivations for consulting can fuel your self-motivation. Reflect on why you chose consulting in the first place—what excites you about this path? Is it the independence, the opportunity to make an impact, or the challenge of solving complex problems? Connecting with your "why" provides a sense of purpose that can keep you motivated, even on tough days.

4. **Celebrating Small Wins:** Consulting is a marathon, not a sprint, and progress can sometimes feel slow. To maintain motivation, take time to celebrate small wins along the way. Whether you sign a new client, receive positive feedback, or hit a personal milestone, acknowledging these achievements reinforces your progress and keeps your momentum going.

AI Reflection Prompt: *What strategies can I use to stay motivated and productive, especially during slower periods in consulting?*

8.4 RESILIENCE: BOUNCING BACK FROM SETBACKS

Resilience—the ability to recover from setbacks and keep moving forward—is a critical mindset trait for consultants.

The consulting path is rarely smooth, involving rejections, project challenges, client conflicts, and periods of uncertainty. Resilience allows you to face these obstacles with a constructive attitude, learn from your experiences, and continue pursuing your goals.

Key Aspects of Resilience in Consulting:

1. **Managing Rejection and Criticism:** Not every client pitch will be successful, and not every project will go as planned. It is essential to develop a thick skin and the ability to handle rejection and criticism without losing confidence. Instead of viewing setbacks as failures, see them as learning opportunities that provide valuable insights for improvement.

2. **Staying Positive and Focused:** Maintaining a positive outlook, even in the face of difficulties, can help you stay resilient. Practice reframing challenges as opportunities to grow and build new skills. Surround yourself with supportive people—whether they are fellow consultants, mentors, or friends—who can offer encouragement and perspective when you need it most.

3. **Practising Self-Care:** Resilience is not just about mental toughness; it also involves taking care of your physical and emotional well-being. Burnout is a real risk in consulting, especially when juggling multiple projects and responsibilities. Make time for self-care practices that replenish your energy, such as exercise, meditation, hobbies, or simply taking breaks. A healthy body and a balanced lifestyle support a resilient mindset.

4. **Developing a Growth Mindset:** Adopting a growth mindset—the belief that abilities and intelligence can be developed through effort and learning—enhances resilience. A growth mindset encourages you to embrace challenges, persist through obstacles, and view effort as a path to mastery. By seeing setbacks as a normal part of the journey, you can maintain a sense of optimism and continue pushing forward.

AI Reflection Prompt: *How can I build resilience to handle client rejections, project setbacks, or periods of low demand in consulting?*

8.5 PROACTIVITY: TAKING CHARGE OF YOUR CONSULTING CAREER

Consulting is not a passive career; it requires a proactive approach to managing your business, seeking out opportunities, and continually refining your skills. Proactivity means taking the initiative rather than waiting for things to happen.

It's about being the driver of your consulting practice, not just a passenger.

Key Aspects of Proactivity in Consulting:

1. **Seeking Opportunities:** As a consultant, you cannot afford to wait for clients to come to you. Proactively seek out opportunities by networking, attending industry events, and remaining visible within your professional community. Regularly reach out to potential clients, follow up on leads, and position yourself as a thought leader through content creation or speaking engagements.

2. **Anticipating Client Needs:** Proactivity also extends to how you engage with clients. Anticipate their needs by staying ahead of industry trends, understanding their challenges, and offering solutions before they ask. By being proactive, you demonstrate value and build stronger client relationships that lead to repeat business and referrals.

3. **Continuous Improvement:** A proactive mindset includes a commitment to continuous improvement. Regularly assess your performance, seek feedback from clients, and look for ways to enhance your services. Stay curious and open to new ideas, and be willing to invest in your professional development to keep your skills sharp and relevant.

4. **Taking Calculated Risks:** Proactivity sometimes involves taking calculated risks, such as entering a new market, expanding your service offerings, or investing in a marketing campaign. Evaluate the potential benefits and downsides, and be willing to step outside your comfort zone when opportunities align with your strategic goals.

AI Reflection Prompt: *What specific actions can I take to be more proactive in seeking opportunities, engaging clients, and refining my consulting services?*

The mindset needed for consulting is characterised by adaptability, self-motivation, resilience, and proactivity. These mental attributes empower you to navigate the complexities of consulting, embrace the challenges of self-employment, and drive your consulting practice forward.

Cultivating the right mindset is not a one-time effort but an ongoing process of self-reflection, learning, and growth.

As you continue your journey towards consulting, focus on developing these mindset traits and aligning your motivations with your consulting goals. A strong mindset supports your professional success and enhances your overall satisfaction and fulfilment as a consultant.

By embracing a consultant's mindset, you can thrive in the dynamic and rewarding world of consulting.

KEY CONCEPTS

Success in consulting depends on cultivating a mindset of adaptability, self-motivation, resilience, and proactivity. These attributes empower you to navigate the dynamic consulting landscape, overcome challenges, and achieve sustainable growth. A strong mindset, combined with clear motivations, serves as the foundation for a thriving and fulfilling consulting career.

8.1 The Importance of Mindset in Consulting

Your mindset shapes how you approach challenges, interact with clients, and sustain success.

A growth-oriented mindset is essential for navigating the complexities of consulting.

Mindset traits such as adaptability, resilience, and self-motivation can be cultivated over time.

8.2 Adaptability: Thriving in a Changing Environment

Embracing Change: View change as an opportunity for growth and skill expansion.

Learning Agility: Stay current with trends, technologies, and methodologies to remain competitive.

Navigating Uncertainty: Cultivate comfort with ambiguity and use it as a catalyst for creativity and problem-solving.

8.3 Self-Motivation: Driving Your Own Success

Setting Clear Goals: Define measurable goals and break them down into actionable steps.

Maintaining Discipline: Build routines that support productivity and adhere to your commitments.

Finding Your "Why": Connect with your deeper motivations to sustain energy and purpose.

Celebrating Small Wins: Acknowledge milestones to maintain momentum and confidence.

8.4 Resilience: Bouncing Back from Setbacks

Managing Rejection: Reframe setbacks as learning opportunities and avoid allowing criticism to derail you.

Staying Positive: Practise optimism and surround yourself with supportive individuals.

Practising Self-Care: Avoid burnout by balancing work with physical and emotional well-being.

Developing a Growth Mindset: View challenges as opportunities for mastery and persistence.

8.5 Proactivity: Taking Charge of Your Consulting Career

Seeking Opportunities: Proactively network, market your services, and remain visible in your industry.

Anticipating Client Needs: Stay ahead of trends and client challenges to demonstrate your value.

Continuous Improvement: Regularly assess and refine your skills, services, and performance.

Taking Calculated Risks: Step outside your comfort zone strategically to explore new opportunities.

REFLECTION

How would you describe your current mindset about pursuing consulting?

What motivates you most about this career path, and what fears or reservations do you have?

EXERCISE: MINDSET AND MOTIVATION JOURNAL

Step 1: Journal Your Motivations. Write a journal entry about your motivations for consulting. Include why you want to pursue this path, what excites you, and what personal or professional goals you hope to achieve.

Step 2: Identify Mindset Barriers. Reflect on any mindset barriers that may be holding you back, such as fear of failure, self-doubt, or concerns about financial instability. Write about these barriers honestly.

Step 3: Reframe Negative Thoughts. For each mindset barrier, write a positive reframe or an action step you can take to address it. For example, if you fear failure, reframe it as an opportunity to learn and grow.

Step 4: Set Mindset Goals. Establish two or three mindset goals that will help you develop a positive and resilient approach to consulting. These may include affirmations, mindfulness practices, or specific actions that align with your motivations.

Step 5: Reflect on Your Progress. Periodically review your journal entries and reflect on your progress. How has your mindset evolved? What steps have you taken to maintain motivation and overcome barriers?

9: RISK TOLERANCE AND FINANCIAL CONSIDERATIONS

One of the most significant aspects of transitioning to solo consulting is the shift from the financial stability of traditional employment to the inherent uncertainties of self-employment.

Consulting offers the potential for higher earnings and greater control over your professional life. However, it also comes with financial risks, including variable income, periods of low client demand, and the responsibility of managing your own benefits.

In this chapter, we will explore how to evaluate your comfort with financial risk, assess your financial readiness for consulting, and provide practical tools to help you prepare for the financial realities of the consulting journey.

9.1 UNDERSTANDING FINANCIAL RISK IN CONSULTING

Consulting is an entrepreneurial endeavour, and like all entrepreneurial ventures, it involves a degree of financial risk.

Unlike traditional employment, where income is typically steady and predictable, consulting income can fluctuate based on factors such as client demand, project timelines, and market conditions. Additionally, consultants are responsible for covering their own health insurance, retirement savings, taxes, and other business expenses.

Understanding the nature of these financial risks is the first step in evaluating your readiness for consulting. It's important to be realistic about the potential for income variability and to have strategies for managing the financial ups and downs. Being aware of the risks enables you to approach consulting with your eyes wide open and make informed decisions about mitigating them.

> **AI Reflection Prompt:** *What are the primary financial risks associated with consulting, and how can I prepare to manage them effectively?*

9.2 EVALUATING YOUR RISK TOLERANCE

Risk tolerance refers to your comfort level with uncertainty and potential financial loss. It's a personal trait that varies from person to person, and understanding your own risk tolerance is crucial for determining whether consulting is the right fit for you. To assess your risk tolerance, consider the following questions:

1. **How do you feel about financial uncertainty?** Reflect on your emotional response to financial uncertainty. Do fluctuations in income cause you significant stress, or are you comfortable with the idea of variable earnings? Your emotional resilience to financial ups and downs is key to your ability to thrive in consulting.
2. **Have you experienced financial risk before?** Consider your past experiences with financial risk. Have you previously been in situations where your income was variable or where you had to make significant financial decisions? How did you handle those experiences? Your past reactions can provide insights into how you might cope with the financial realities of consulting.
3. **What is your current financial situation?** Evaluate your current financial health, including your savings, debt levels, and overall financial stability. Are you able to afford financial

risks, or do you rely heavily on a consistent income to meet your obligations? Understanding your financial baseline will help you gauge how much risk you can reasonably take on.

4. **What are your financial priorities and obligations?** Consider your financial responsibilities, such as mortgage payments, family expenses, and student loans. Are these obligations manageable within a consulting context, or do they require the security of a regular paycheck? Assessing your financial commitments will help you determine how much risk is acceptable.

5. **Are you willing to adjust your lifestyle?** Consulting may require lifestyle adjustments, especially in the early stages. Are you prepared to reduce discretionary spending, live on a tighter budget, or make short-term sacrifices to build your consulting business? Your willingness to adapt your lifestyle can influence your overall risk tolerance.

AI Reflection Prompt: *How can I assess my comfort level with financial uncertainty and determine whether consulting aligns with my risk tolerance?*

9.3 ASSESSING YOUR FINANCIAL READINESS FOR CONSULTING

Beyond understanding your risk tolerance, it is important to assess your financial readiness for consulting. This involves evaluating your financial reserves, income requirements, and the costs associated with starting and running a consulting business.

Key Steps to Assess Financial Readiness:

1. **Calculate Your Monthly Living Expenses:** Start by calculating your current monthly living expenses, including housing, utilities, groceries, transportation, insurance, debt payments, and discretionary spending. This will give you a clear picture of your baseline financial needs.

2. **Estimate Your Business Expenses:** Next, estimate the costs associated with running your consulting business. This can include expenses such as marketing, software and tools,

professional development, travel, office supplies, and legal or accounting services. Understanding these costs will help you set realistic financial goals for your consulting income.

3. **Determine Your Minimum Income Requirement:** Combine your monthly living and business expenses to determine your minimum income requirement. This figure represents the monthly amount you need to earn to cover personal and business costs. Setting this baseline is important so you have a clear target for your consulting income.

4. **Build a Financial Buffer:** A financial buffer, or emergency fund, is a crucial safety net for consultants. Ideally, you should have at least three to six months' worth of living and business expenses saved before transitioning into consulting. This buffer will help you manage periods of low income, unexpected expenses, or delays in client payments, thereby reducing the financial stress associated with consulting.

5. **Plan for Taxes and Benefits:** As a consultant, you are responsible for paying your own taxes, including income tax. It is important to set aside a portion of your income for taxes and to stay organised with your financial records. Additionally, plan for your own benefits, such as health insurance, retirement savings, and paid time off, as these will not be provided by an employer.

   AI Reflection Prompt: *What steps can I take to evaluate my current financial situation, including savings, debt, and income needs, to determine my readiness for consulting?*

9.4 TOOLS AND STRATEGIES FOR MANAGING FINANCIAL RISK

Managing financial risk in consulting involves proactive planning, disciplined budgeting, and strategic financial management. Here are some tools and strategies to help you navigate the financial aspects of consulting:

1. **Create a Detailed Budget:** Develop a comprehensive budget that includes personal and business expenses. Use this budget to track your spending, identify areas where you can cut costs, and ensure you stay within your income limits. Regularly review and adjust your budget as your income and expenses fluctuate.

2. **Implement a Cash Flow Management System:** Cash flow is the lifeblood of any consulting business. Implement a system that helps you track incoming payments, outgoing expenses, and overall profitability. Consider using financial software or apps that offer cash flow projections and alerts to help you stay on top of your finances.

3. **Diversify Your Income Streams:** Diversifying your income streams can help reduce the impact of variability in consulting income. Consider offering a mix of services, such as project-based work, retainer agreements, workshops, or online courses. By diversifying your revenue sources, you can create a more stable financial foundation for your consulting practice.

4. **Set Up a Separate Business Account:** Keep your personal and business finances separate by setting up a dedicated business bank account. This will help you better manage your consulting income, track business expenses, and simplify your tax preparation. It also creates a clear distinction between your personal and professional finances, thereby reducing the risk of overspending.

5. **Regularly Review Your Financial Health:** Make it a habit to regularly review your financial health, including your income, expenses, savings, and progress towards financial goals. Regular reviews will help you stay proactive in managing your finances, identify any potential issues early, and make informed decisions about your consulting business.

AI Reflection Prompt: *What tools or systems can I use to track and control my consulting finances effectively?*

9.5 CREATING A FINANCIAL CONTINGENCY PLAN

A financial contingency plan is a proactive approach to managing financial risks and ensuring you are prepared for potential challenges. Your contingency plan should outline the steps to take if your consulting income falls short of your needs or unexpected expenses arise.

Key Elements of a Financial Contingency Plan:

1. **Identify Potential Risks:** Start by identifying potential financial risks, such as losing a major client, experiencing a prolonged slow period, or facing unexpected business expenses. Understanding these risks allows you to develop strategies to mitigate them.
2. **Set Financial Triggers:** Establish financial triggers that prompt you to take action. For example, if your income drops below a certain threshold for consecutive months, this could trigger a review of your expenses, adjustments to your marketing efforts, or a temporary return to part-time employment.
3. **Outline Action Steps:** Define clear action steps for each financial trigger. These might include cutting non-essential expenses, ramping up business development activities, or tapping into your financial buffer. Having a predefined plan reduces the stress of decision-making during challenging times and provides a roadmap for navigating financial difficulties.
4. **Reevaluate and Adjust as Needed:** A financial contingency plan is not static; it should evolve as your consulting business grows and your financial situation changes. Regularly reevaluate your plan, adjust your financial triggers, and update your action steps to reflect your current circumstances.

> **AI Reflection Prompt:** *What should my financial contingency plan include to help me navigate potential challenges, such as losing a client or facing unexpected expenses?*

Evaluating your risk tolerance and financial readiness is critical in determining whether consulting is the right path for you. You can approach consulting with greater confidence and preparedness by understanding your comfort level with financial uncertainty, assessing your current financial situation, and implementing tools and strategies to manage financial risks.

Consulting offers the potential for financial independence and the opportunity to shape your own professional destiny, but it requires careful financial planning and a proactive approach to managing variability. Use the insights and tools from this chapter to build a solid financial foundation, reduce your exposure to financial risks, and set yourself up for a successful consulting journey.

KEY CONCEPTS

Understanding your risk tolerance and financial readiness is essential for transitioning to consulting. By evaluating your comfort with uncertainty, preparing financially, and implementing risk management tools, you can confidently navigate the financial challenges of consulting. A strong financial foundation and proactive planning ensure long-term success and stability in your consulting journey.

9.1 Understanding Financial Risk in Consulting

Consulting income is variable, influenced by client demand, project timelines, and market conditions.

Consultants cover their own benefits, taxes, and business expenses, adding to their financial responsibility.

Awareness of financial risks allows for informed decisions and strategies to mitigate variability.

9.2 Evaluating Your Risk Tolerance

Comfort with Financial Uncertainty: Assess how fluctuations in income impact your stress levels.

Experience with Financial Risk: Reflect on how you have handled variable income or significant financial decisions in the past.

Current Financial Situation: Evaluate your savings, debt levels, and overall financial stability.

Financial Priorities and Obligations: Consider commitments such as mortgage payments or family expenses.

Lifestyle Adjustments: Determine your willingness to reduce expenses or adapt your lifestyle in the early stages of consulting.

9.3 Assessing Your Financial Readiness

Monthly Living Expenses: Calculate your baseline financial needs.

Business Expenses: Estimate the costs associated with running a consulting business (e.g., marketing, tools, travel).

Minimum Income Requirement: Combine personal and business expenses to set a monthly income target.

Financial Buffer: Save 3–6 months' worth of living and business expenses as a safety net.

Taxes and Benefits: Plan for self-managed taxes, insurance, and retirement savings.

9.4 Tools and Strategies for Managing Financial Risk

Budgeting: Track and adjust your spending for both personal and business expenses.

Cash Flow Management: Use tools or software to monitor income, expenses, and profitability.

Diversifying Income Streams: Reduce income variability by offering multiple services (e.g., retainers, courses, workshops).

Separate Business Accounts: Keep personal and business finances distinct for better management.

Financial Reviews: Regularly evaluate your income, expenses, and progress toward your financial goals.

9.5 Creating a Financial Contingency Plan

Identify Risks: Anticipate potential challenges, such as losing clients or experiencing slow periods.

Set Financial Triggers: Define income thresholds that will prompt corrective actions.

Action Steps: Predefine steps such as expense reductions, increased marketing, or temporary part-time work.

Ongoing Adjustments: Regularly update your contingency plan to align with current circumstances.

REFLECTION

How comfortable are you with the financial risks associated with consulting?

What steps can you take to mitigate these risks and ensure financial stability?

EXERCISE: FINANCIAL READINESS ASSESSMENT

Step 1: Evaluate Your Financial Situation. List your current financial assets, including savings, investments, and any other sources of income. Then, list your financial obligations, such as debts, monthly expenses, and upcoming major costs.

Step 2: Assess Your Financial Buffer. Calculate how many months of living expenses your current savings could cover if your consulting income were to vary. Aim for at least three to six months as a baseline financial buffer.

Step 3: Identify Financial Risks. Identify the primary financial risks associated with transitioning to consulting, such as income variability, initial startup costs, and potential slow periods. Write these down in a clear list.

Step 4: Develop a Risk Mitigation Plan. For each financial risk, outline a strategy to mitigate it. This could include building a larger emergency fund, securing a line of credit, creating a budget with reduced expenses, or starting consulting part-time while maintaining your current income.

Step 5: Reflect on Your Financial Readiness. Summarise your financial readiness in a brief reflection. How prepared do you feel financially to pursue consulting? How can you enhance your financial security and comfort with risk?

10: LIFESTYLE FIT: CONSULTING AND WORK-LIFE BALANCE

One of the most appealing aspects of consulting is the promise of greater control over your time and work-life balance. However, the reality of consulting can be complex, and it is essential to consider how this career path aligns with your personal lifestyle and priorities.

Consulting offers flexibility but also requires discipline, effective time management, and the ability to set boundaries between work and personal life.

This chapter will discuss how consulting can impact your lifestyle and work-life balance. It will help you envision the day-to-day realities and personal trade-offs involved in a consulting career.

10.1 THE FLEXIBILITY OF CONSULTING: A DOUBLE-EDGED SWORD

Flexibility is one of the most touted benefits of consulting. As a consultant, you have the autonomy to set your own schedule, choose where you work, and decide which projects to take on.

This flexibility can provide significant lifestyle benefits, such as spending more time with family, pursuing personal interests, or avoiding the constraints of a traditional office environment.

However, flexibility can also be a double-edged sword. Without the structure of a typical 9-to-5 job, it is easy for work to bleed into personal time. The freedom to set your own hours can lead to irregular work patterns, long days, or difficulty disconnecting from work.

The challenge for consultants is to harness the benefits of flexibility while maintaining a healthy work-life balance.

Key Considerations for Managing Flexibility in Consulting

1. **Setting Boundaries:** Establishing clear boundaries between work and personal time is crucial for maintaining balance. This might involve setting specific work hours, creating a dedicated workspace, and resisting the urge to check emails or work on projects during personal time. By defining when and where you work, you can create a separation that helps protect your personal life.

2. **Prioritising Your Time:** With the autonomy of consulting comes the responsibility to manage your time effectively. Prioritise your tasks, focus on high-impact activities, and avoid overcommitting to projects. Use tools like time-blocking or project management software to stay organised and ensure that your work does not encroach on your personal time.

3. **Embracing Flexibility Intentionally:** Rather than letting flexibility dictate your schedule, use it intentionally to enhance your lifestyle. Plan work around important personal commitments, take breaks when needed, and leverage the freedom of consulting to create a rhythm that suits you. Remember that flexibility is a tool to be used purposefully, not a licence to work without structure.

AI Reflection Prompts: *How can I intentionally use the flexibility of consulting to align my work schedule with my personal priorities?*

I struggle with time management. Can you suggest strategies to help me manage my consulting schedule effectively?

10.2 THE DAY-TO-DAY REALITIES OF CONSULTING

Consulting can vary significantly from day to day, depending on the nature of your projects, client needs, and personal preferences. While the lack of routine can be invigorating, it can also present challenges for those who thrive on consistency.

Understanding the day-to-day realities of consulting can help you prepare for the dynamic nature of this career.

Common Day-to-Day Activities in Consulting

1. **Client Work:** The bulk of your time as a consultant will be spent on client work, which may include research, analysis, problem-solving, and project management. Depending on your niche, this could involve deep technical work, strategic advisory, or hands-on implementation. Each day may bring different tasks, and your ability to adapt to each client's needs is essential.

2. **Business Development:** Much of your time will also be dedicated to business development activities such as networking, marketing, proposal writing, and pitching to potential clients. This ongoing effort ensures a steady pipeline of work and requires consistent attention alongside your client projects.

3. **Administrative Tasks:** Running a consulting business involves various administrative tasks, including invoicing, bookkeeping, scheduling, and responding to emails. While these tasks may not be the most glamorous part of consulting, they are necessary for keeping your business running smoothly.

4. **Professional Development:** Staying current in your field is critical for maintaining your consulting value. Allocate time for professional development activities, such as attending webinars, reading industry publications, or pursuing certifications. Continuous learning helps you stay competitive and offers opportunities to expand your service offerings.

AI Reflection Prompts: *Which common consulting activities should I focus on, based on the challenges I might face as a solo consultant?*

How can I consistently integrate professional development into my schedule to remain relevant and competitive in my field?

10.3 PERSONAL TRADE-OFFS IN CONSULTING

While consulting offers many advantages, it also comes with personal trade-offs that can impact your lifestyle. Understanding these trade-offs will help you make a more informed decision about whether consulting aligns with your overall vision for your life.

1. **Income Variability:** As discussed in the previous chapter, income variability is a key trade-off in consulting. Financial unpredictability can affect lifestyle choices, such as planning vacations, making large purchases, or committing to long-term financial obligations. Consultants must be comfortable navigating these uncertainties and may need to adjust their lifestyle accordingly.

2. **Blurred Work-Life Boundaries:** The flexibility of consulting can sometimes lead to blurred boundaries between work and personal life. Without clear separation, it is easy to work late into the evening or over weekends, which can lead to burnout. Proactively setting boundaries and managing your time is critical to maintaining a sustainable work-life balance.

3. **Isolation and Lack of Team Interaction:** Consulting can be isolating, especially if you work independently or remotely. The lack of daily interaction with colleagues can be a significant adjustment for those used to the social aspects of a traditional workplace. Building a network of fellow consultants, joining professional groups, or working from co-working spaces can help mitigate feelings of isolation.

4. **Responsibility for All Aspects of Your Business:** As a solo consultant, you are responsible for every aspect of your business, from delivering client work to handling finances and marketing. This can be both empowering and overwhelming.

The additional responsibilities can consume time and mental energy, leaving less room for personal pursuits. Consider whether you are comfortable wearing multiple hats or if you might benefit from outsourcing certain tasks.

5. **Inconsistent Workload:** Consulting can involve cycles of feast and famine, with periods of intense work followed by lulls. This inconsistency can disrupt your personal plans and make it difficult to maintain a regular routine. Developing strategies to manage your workload, such as scheduling downtime or balancing overlapping projects, can help smooth out these fluctuations.

AI Reflection Prompts: *What financial practices can I adopt to handle the income variability of consulting effectively?*

Consulting can be isolating. What steps can I take to build a strong network or find community support as a solo consultant?

10.4 ENVISIONING YOUR IDEAL CONSULTING LIFESTYLE

Imagine your ideal consulting day to determine whether consulting fits your desired lifestyle. Consider factors such as your preferred work hours, the types of projects you want to work on, and how you will balance work and personal commitments.

Visualising your ideal consulting lifestyle can help you set realistic expectations and identify any adjustments you might need to make.

Questions to Envision Your Ideal Consulting Lifestyle

1. **What Does Your Perfect Workday Look Like?** Imagine your ideal consulting workday. Are you working from home, in a coffee shop, or a co-working space? Do you start your day early or prefer a more flexible schedule? Visualising your perfect day can help you design a consulting practice that aligns with your lifestyle goals.

2. **How Do You Balance Work and Personal Commitments?** Consider how you will integrate work with personal

commitments such as family time, exercise, hobbies, or travel. What boundaries will you set to protect your personal time, and how will you ensure that consulting enhances, rather than detracts from, your overall quality of life?

3. **What Lifestyle Priorities Are Non-Negotiable?** Identify your non-negotiable lifestyle priorities—those aspects of your life that are most important to you and that you are unwilling to compromise. This could include spending time with loved ones, maintaining a specific fitness routine, or having the flexibility to travel. Ensure that your consulting practice is designed to support these priorities.

4. **How Will You Handle Busy Periods and Downtime?** Plan for the inevitable ebbs and flows of consulting work. How will you manage periods of high workload without sacrificing your personal well-being? Conversely, how will you make the most of slower periods to recharge, pursue professional development, or focus on business growth?

AI Reflection Prompt: *During slower consulting periods, how can I stay productive while also recharging and preparing for future work?*

10.5 STRATEGIES FOR MAINTAINING WORK-LIFE BALANCE IN CONSULTING

Maintaining work-life balance in consulting requires intentionality and a proactive approach. Here are some strategies to help you create and sustain a balanced lifestyle:

1. **Set Clear Boundaries:** Define clear boundaries between work and personal time. This could include setting specific work hours, turning off notifications outside those hours, and creating a dedicated workspace that separates work from leisure activities.

2. **Practice Time Management:** Effective time management is essential for balancing the demands of consulting. Use tools like calendars, to-do lists, and project management software to organise your tasks and prioritise your time. Focus on high-

impact activities and avoid the temptation to overextend yourself.

3. **Schedule Downtime:** Just as you schedule work tasks, schedule downtime and personal activities. Make time for self-care, exercise, and relaxation to prevent burnout. Treat personal commitments with the same importance as client meetings or deadlines.

4. **Leverage Support Networks:** Build a support network of fellow consultants, mentors, friends, or family members who can encourage you, offer advice, and provide perspective. A support system can help you navigate the challenges of consulting and maintain a sense of connection.

5. **Be Mindful of Your Energy Levels:** Pay attention to your energy levels throughout the day and plan your work accordingly. Tackle high-concentration tasks when you're most alert and save less demanding activities for when your energy dips. Being mindful of your energy helps you work more efficiently and reduces stress.

AI Reflection Prompts: *What time management tools or techniques would help me balance consulting work with personal commitments?*

Can you suggest ways to incorporate self-care and personal activities into my consulting schedule to avoid burnout?

Consulting offers the flexibility to design a work-life balance that aligns with your personal priorities, but it also requires discipline, boundary-setting, and self-awareness.

By understanding the lifestyle implications of consulting and proactively managing your time and commitments, you can create a consulting practice that enhances your quality of life.

As you consider whether consulting is right for you, reflect on how it aligns with your desired lifestyle and the trade-offs you are willing to make.

Consulting is not just a career choice; it is a way of living that can bring fulfilment, autonomy, and balance—provided you approach it with intention and clarity about your personal values and goals.

KEY CONCEPTS

Consulting provides the flexibility and autonomy to design a work-life balance that aligns with your personal priorities, but it requires intentionality, discipline, and boundary-setting to avoid pitfalls. By understanding the lifestyle implications and proactively managing your time and commitments, you can create a sustainable consulting practice that enhances both your professional success and personal fulfilment.

10.1 The Flexibility of Consulting: A Double-Edged Sword

Benefits of Flexibility: Autonomy to set your schedule, choose projects, and work from preferred locations.

Challenges of Flexibility: Without boundaries, work can spill into personal time, leading to long hours or irregular work patterns.

Managing Flexibility:

- Set clear boundaries between work and personal time.
- Prioritise tasks and avoid overcommitting.
- Intentionally use flexibility to align work with personal commitments.

10.2 The Day-to-Day Realities of Consulting

Client Work: Focus on delivering solutions through research, analysis, and project management.

Business Development: Ongoing efforts to market services, network, and secure new clients.

Administrative Tasks: Managing invoicing, scheduling, and other business operations.

Professional Development: Continuous learning to maintain relevance and expand offerings.

10.3 Personal Trade-Offs in Consulting

Income Variability: Requires managing financial unpredictability and adjusting lifestyle accordingly.

Blurred Boundaries: Risk of work encroaching on personal life without clear separation.

Isolation: Limited daily interaction with colleagues, which can be mitigated by building a support network or using coworking spaces.

Multiple Responsibilities: Solo consultants manage all aspects of their business, which can be both empowering and time-consuming.

Inconsistent Workload: Fluctuations in workload necessitate strategies to balance intense periods with downtime.

10.4 Envisioning Your Ideal Consulting Lifestyle

Perfect Workday: Define your preferred working hours, environment, and routine.

Work-Life Integration: Plan how to balance consulting with personal commitments, such as family, hobbies, and travel.

Lifestyle Non-Negotiables: Identify priorities that must be maintained, such as fitness routines or time with loved ones.

Managing Peaks and Lulls: Develop plans for handling busy periods and make productive use of downtime.

10.5 Strategies for Maintaining Work-Life Balance

Set Clear Boundaries: Define your working hours and create a dedicated workspace to separate work from personal life.

Practice Time Management: Use calendars and project management tools to organise tasks and avoid overextending yourself.

Schedule Downtime: Prioritise self-care and personal activities to prevent burnout.

Leverage Support Networks: Build connections with peers, mentors, and loved ones for encouragement and advice.

Mind Energy Levels: Align high-concentration tasks with peak energy times and reserve less demanding work for slower periods.

EXERCISE: LIFESTYLE ALIGNMENT VISUALISATION

Step 1: Visualise Your Ideal Day as a Consultant. Close your eyes and take a few moments to visualise your ideal day as a consultant. Consider your working hours, the types of projects you are engaged in, your work environment, and how you balance personal and professional commitments.

Step 2: Write Your Vision. Write down your vision of this ideal day in detail. Include specifics about when you start work, how you structure your day, your flexibility, and how you make time for personal activities, family, or other interests.

Step 3: Compare to Your Current Lifestyle. Compare your vision to your current lifestyle. Identify the key differences and what changes would be necessary for you to achieve your ideal work-life balance as a consultant.

Step 4: Plan for Lifestyle Adjustments. Based on your comparison, outline any adjustments or preparations needed to align your lifestyle with your consulting goals. This may involve setting boundaries, organising your workspace, planning your schedule, or discussing changes with family or partners.

Step 5: Reflect on Lifestyle Fit. Reflect on how consulting aligns with your desired lifestyle. Are the necessary changes feasible and appealing? How confident do you feel about achieving the work-life balance you envision through consulting?

PART 3: EXPLORING THE MARKET AND IDENTIFYING YOUR NICHE

The best way to find yourself is to lose yourself in the service of others.

11: FINDING YOUR UNIQUE VALUE PROPOSITION

One of the most critical steps in establishing yourself as a consultant is defining your unique value proposition (UVP).

In a competitive consulting market, your UVP sets you apart and helps potential clients understand why they should choose you over other consultants. It clarifies what makes you unique, the specific skills and expertise you bring to the table, and the problems you are best equipped to solve.

In this chapter, we will guide you through the process of defining your UVP, emphasising the importance of differentiation and how to effectively communicate your value to prospective clients.

11.1 UNDERSTANDING THE UNIQUE VALUE PROPOSITION

Your UVP is essentially your promise to clients—it articulates the specific benefits and value they will receive from working with you. It's not just about listing your skills or qualifications; it's about identifying the distinct ways you can solve clients' problems better, faster, or more effectively than others.

A strong UVP answers the fundamental question: *Why should a client hire you?*

A well-defined UVP serves several purposes:

- **Differentiation:** It sets you apart from competitors by highlighting what makes your consulting services unique.
- **Clarity:** It provides clarity to potential clients about what you offer and the results they can expect.
- **Focus:** It helps you stay focused on your strengths and target the right market segments where your expertise is most valued.
- **Marketing Tool:** A clear UVP is a powerful marketing tool that you can use in your pitches, on your website, and in promotional materials to attract and engage clients.

AI Reflection Prompts: *Based on my skills and experiences [insert your skills/experiences], can you help me identify what might differentiate me as a consultant in my field?*

If I want to emphasise [insert specific expertise or achievement], how can I frame it as part of my unique value proposition to appeal to potential clients?

11.2 STEPS TO DEFINE YOUR UNIQUE VALUE PROPOSITION

Defining your UVP involves introspection, market research, and a deep understanding of your skills and the problems you can solve. Here's a step-by-step guide to help you develop a compelling UVP:

Step 1: Identify Your Core Skills and Expertise

Start by making a comprehensive list of your core skills and areas of expertise. Think about your technical knowledge, industry experience, specific methodologies, and any unique approaches you bring to your work. Be as specific as possible—what are you particularly good at? What do others consistently seek your advice on?

Consider these questions to help identify your core skills:

- What are your top technical skills?
- Which industries or sectors do you have the most experience in?
- Are there specific tools, technologies, or methodologies where you excel?
- Do you have any unique qualifications, certifications, or awards that enhance your credibility?

Step 2: Understand the Problems You Solve

Next, shift your focus to the problems you are uniquely positioned to solve. Clients hire consultants not just for their skills but for the solutions they provide.

Reflect on the types of challenges or pain points your skills can address. This could range from technical issues, such as optimising a complex system, to strategic challenges, like guiding a company through digital transformation.

To identify the problems you solve, consider:

- What common challenges do your past employers or clients face that you have successfully addressed?
- What specific outcomes or improvements have you delivered in your previous roles?
- Are there recurring themes or patterns in the types of problems you solve?

Step 3: Research Your Market and Competition

Understanding market demand and your competition is crucial for defining a Unique Value Proposition (UVP) that resonates. Research your target market to identify the current needs and pain points that align with your skills.

Additionally, analyse your competitors: what services do they offer, and how do they position themselves? Look for gaps in the market that your unique skills can fill.

Key aspects to research include:

- Who are your potential clients, and what are their pressing challenges?
- What solutions are your competitors offering, and how are they positioned?
- Are there unmet needs in the market that your skills can address?

Step 4: Define Your Differentiators

Based on your skills, the problems you solve, and your market research, identify the key differentiators that set you apart. These differentiators could include specialised expertise, a unique approach, proven results, or exceptional client service.

The goal is to pinpoint what makes you distinctly valuable to your target clients. Questions to help define your differentiators:

- What do you offer that others don't?
- How do you deliver value differently from your competitors?
- What unique insights or approaches do you bring to the table?

Step 5: Craft Your Unique Value Proposition Statement

With a clear understanding of your skills, the problems you solve, and your differentiators, it's time to craft your UVP statement.

Your UVP should be concise, specific, and client-focused, clearly communicating the value you deliver. A strong UVP statement includes three main elements:

- **Who you serve:** Identify your target clients or market segment.
- **What you do:** Clearly state the specific service or solution you provide.

- **Why it's valuable:** Highlight the benefits and outcomes your clients can expect.

Example UVP Template: "I help target clients achieve specific outcomes by providing your unique solution or approach, which explains why it's better or different."

Example UVP Statement: "I help mid-sized tech companies optimise their software development processes by implementing agile methodologies, reducing project timelines by 30% and increasing team productivity."

> **AI Reflection Prompts:** *Here are my top technical and soft skills: [insert skills]. Can you help me determine which ones are most relevant for consulting and how to highlight them effectively?*
>
> *I want to create a UVP statement using this template: "I help [target clients] achieve [specific outcome] by providing [unique solution]." Can you help me refine it with this information: [insert your initial draft or key details]?*

11.3 THE IMPORTANCE OF DIFFERENTIATION IN CONSULTING

Differentiation is at the heart of your UVP. In a crowded consulting market, standing out is essential for attracting the right clients and commanding premium rates. Differentiation goes beyond your skills; it encompasses your approach, your client experience, and the specific results you deliver.

Key Aspects of Differentiation in Consulting:

1. **Niche Expertise:** Specialising in a niche area can set you apart from generalist consultants. Whether it's a particular industry, technology, or type of problem, niche expertise positions you as a go-to expert and helps you attract clients who need your specific skills.
2. **Unique Approach or Methodology:** How you deliver your services can be a powerful differentiator. Do you have a unique process, framework, or methodology that enhances results?

Highlighting your distinctive approach can make your services more appealing to clients looking for innovative solutions.

3. **Proven Results and Case Studies:** Demonstrating a track record of success through case studies, testimonials, and quantifiable results builds credibility and sets you apart. Clients want to see evidence that you can deliver on your promises, and showcasing past successes is a compelling way to differentiate yourself.

4. **Client Experience:** Differentiation is not just about what you do but also how you do it. Providing exceptional client service, being responsive, and creating a positive client experience can be significant differentiators that encourage repeat business and referrals.

AI Reflection Prompt: *My niche expertise is [insert niche], and I use [insert unique approach/methodology]. How can I clearly communicate these as key differentiators to clients?*

11.4 COMMUNICATING YOUR UNIQUE VALUE PROPOSITION

Once you have defined your UVP, it's important to communicate it effectively across all client touchpoints. Your UVP should be prominently featured in your marketing materials, including your website, LinkedIn profile, proposals, and pitches. Consistency is key—ensure that your UVP is clearly conveyed in all interactions with potential clients.

Tips for Communicating Your UVP:

1. **Website and Online Presence:** Your website is often the first point of contact with potential clients. Clearly display your UVP on your homepage, services page, and about section. Use compelling language that speaks directly to your target audience's needs.

2. **Networking and Introductions:** When introducing yourself at networking events or meetings, use your UVP to succinctly explain what you do and the value you provide. A clear and

concise UVP helps others understand your expertise quickly and makes it easier for them to refer you to potential clients.

3. **Proposals and Pitches:** Tailor your UVP to each specific client when writing proposals or delivering pitches. Highlight how your unique skills and approach directly address their needs and explain why you are the best choice for the project.

4. **Social Media and Content Marketing:** Use your UVP as a foundation for your content marketing strategy. Share insights, case studies, and success stories that reinforce your UVP and demonstrate your expertise. Consistently align your content with the unique value you offer to build your brand presence.

AI Reflection Prompt: *I want to create content like blogs or case studies that align with my UVP. Based on my focus area [insert area], what types of stories or topics would help reinforce my credibility?*

11.5 REFINING AND EVOLVING YOUR UVP

Your UVP is not static: it should evolve as your skills develop, market needs change, and you gain more experience. Regularly review and refine your UVP to ensure it remains relevant and aligned with your consulting business. Seek feedback from clients, monitor market trends, and stay attuned to how your competitors are positioning themselves. By continuously refining your UVP, you can maintain a strong market presence and adapt to shifting client needs.

Defining your unique value proposition is a foundational step in establishing your consulting business. A well-crafted UVP differentiates you from competitors, communicates the specific value you offer, and helps attract the right clients. By identifying your core skills, understanding the problems you solve, and clearly articulating your unique value, you position yourself as a sought-after consultant in your niche.

As you move forward, keep your UVP at the forefront of your marketing and client interactions. Use it as a guide to focus your efforts, tailor your services, and continually reinforce the distinct value you bring to your clients. A strong UVP is more than a statement: it's a strategic tool that drives your consulting success.

KEY CONCEPTS

1. Understanding the Unique Value Proposition (UVP)

Your UVP answers: *Why should a client hire you?*

It differentiates you, provides clarity to clients, and helps you focus on your strengths and target markets.

A clear UVP serves as a powerful marketing tool.

2. Steps to Define Your UVP

Identify Core Skills: Highlight your technical expertise, industry experience, and unique methodologies.

Understand Problems You Solve: Define the specific challenges and pain points you are uniquely equipped to address.

Research Market and Competition: Analyse client needs, competitor offerings, and the gaps your skills can fill.

Define Differentiators: Pinpoint what sets you apart (e.g., niche expertise, proven results, unique methods).

Craft Your UVP Statement: Create a concise, client-focused statement that defines who you help, what you do, and why it is valuable.

3. Importance of Differentiation in Consulting

Niche Expertise: Specialising positions you as a go-to expert.

Unique Approach: A proprietary methodology or framework adds appeal.

Proven Results: Case studies and quantifiable success build credibility.

Client Experience: Exceptional service fosters referrals and repeat business.

4. Communicating Your UVP

Website and Online Presence: Display your UVP prominently with language tailored to your target audience.

Networking and Introductions: Use your UVP to succinctly explain your value in meetings and events.

Proposals and Pitches: Customise your UVP to address each client's specific needs.

Social Media and Content Marketing: Share content that reinforces your UVP and showcases your expertise.

5. Refining and Evolving Your UVP

Regularly update your UVP based on feedback, market trends, and new skills.

Ensure it remains aligned with client needs and industry shifts.

6. Crafting a UVP Statement

A strong UVP statement includes:

Who you serve: Define your target clients.

What you do: State your services or solutions.

Why it is valuable: Highlight benefits and outcomes.

7. UVP as a Strategic Tool

Use your UVP to guide marketing, focus your services, and reinforce the value you bring to clients.

EXERCISE: CRAFTING YOUR UNIQUE VALUE PROPOSITION (UVP)

Step 1: Identify Your Key Strengths. List your top strengths, skills, and experiences that are relevant to consulting. Include both technical skills and soft skills such as communication, problem-solving, or leadership.

Step 2: Define the Problems You Solve. Consider the problems your target clients face that you are uniquely equipped to solve. Be specific about the pain points or challenges you can address through your consulting services.

Step 3: Highlight What Sets You Apart. Reflect on what differentiates you from other consultants in your field. This could be your industry experience, a specialised skill set, a unique methodology, or a distinctive perspective.

Step 4: Create Your UVP Statement. Combine the insights from the previous steps into a concise UVP statement. Your statement should clearly articulate who you help, what problems you solve, and why you are the best choice.

Example of a UVP Statement: "I help small technology startups streamline their product development processes, leveraging my 10 years of experience in agile project management to reduce time to market and enhance product quality."

Step 5: Test and Refine Your UVP. Share your UVP statement with trusted colleagues, mentors, or potential clients for feedback. Refine your statement based on their input to ensure it resonates and clearly communicates your unique value.

Step 6: Reflect on Your UVP. Consider how confident you feel in your UVP and how well it aligns with your skills and goals. How does this UVP guide your next steps in defining your consulting services and marketing strategy?

12: UNDERSTANDING MARKET DEMAND FOR YOUR EXPERTISE

I dentifying and understanding market demand for your consulting services is a crucial step in building a successful consulting practice. Knowing where your skills are needed, who your potential clients are, and how to position yourself in the market can make the difference between a thriving business and a struggling one.

In this chapter, we will provide a basic framework for conducting market research to assess the demand for your expertise. This includes identifying potential clients, exploring relevant industries, and evaluating how your unique skills fit into the current market landscape.

12.1 THE IMPORTANCE OF MARKET RESEARCH IN CONSULTING

Market research is the process of gathering, analysing, and interpreting information about a market, including insights about potential clients, competitors, and industry trends. For consultants, market research serves several key purposes:

- **Validation:** It helps validate the demand for your consulting services, ensuring that there is a market need for what you offer.

- **Targeting:** It assists in identifying and targeting the right clients and industries where your expertise can have the most impact.
- **Positioning:** It enables you to position your services effectively, differentiating yourself from competitors and aligning your offerings with market needs.
- **Strategic Planning:** It provides insights that inform your business strategy, including pricing, marketing, and service development.

Conducting thorough market research allows you to make data-driven decisions about your consulting business, reducing risks and increasing your chances of success.

> **AI Reflection Prompt:** *Can you guide me on how to conduct market research to validate demand for my consulting services and identify industries where my expertise would be most impactful?*

12.2 STEPS TO CONDUCT MARKET RESEARCH FOR CONSULTING

Conducting market research does not have to be overly complex or time-consuming. By following a structured approach, you can gather the key insights needed to assess market demand for your expertise. Here's a step-by-step framework to guide your market research efforts:

Step 1: Define Your Target Market. The first step in market research is defining your target market. This involves identifying the specific clients or industries that are most likely to need your consulting services. Start by considering your existing knowledge and experience:

- **Industry Focus:** Identify industries where your skills are most applicable. For example, if you specialise in data analytics, industries such as finance, healthcare, and technology might be relevant. Consider both broad industries and niche sectors that could benefit from your expertise.
- **Client Size:** Determine the size of the clients you want to work with. Are you targeting small businesses, mid-sized

companies, large enterprises, or startups? The needs and budgets of these clients can vary significantly, so it's important to align your services with the appropriate client size.

- **Client Characteristics:** Define specific characteristics of your ideal clients, such as their geographic location, business stage, or the specific challenges they face. The more specific you are, the easier it will be to tailor your marketing and outreach efforts.

Step 2: Identify Market Needs and Pain Points. Once you have defined your target market, the next step is to identify the specific needs and pain points within that market. Understanding the challenges your potential clients face allows you to tailor your services to address those issues effectively.

- **Client Interviews:** Conduct informal interviews or surveys with potential clients to gather insights into their current challenges and needs. Ask open-ended questions to uncover pain points and explore how your skills could help solve their problems.
- **Industry Reports and Publications:** Review industry reports, white papers, and publications to gain an understanding of broader trends and issues affecting your target market. Look for recurring themes that align with your expertise.
- **Online Forums and Social Media:** Participate in online forums, LinkedIn groups, and other social media platforms where your target clients are active. Pay attention to the questions and discussions to identify common challenges and concerns.

Step 3: Analyse Your Competitors. Understanding your competition is a key component of market research. Analysing other consultants who operate in your niche can provide valuable insights into what works, what doesn't, and how you can differentiate yourself.

- **Identify Competitors:** Begin by identifying your main competitors. These could be other solo consultants, small consulting firms, or even larger companies that offer similar services.
- **Evaluate Their Offerings:** Review your competitors' service offerings, pricing, marketing strategies, and client base. What services do they provide, and how do they position themselves? Are there any gaps in their offerings that you could fill?
- **Assess Their Strengths and Weaknesses:** Identify your competitors' strengths and weaknesses. What do they do well, and where do they fall short? Use this information to refine your own unique value proposition and identify opportunities for differentiation.

Step 4: Assess Market Demand and Trends. To fully understand market demand, it's important to evaluate current trends that may impact the need for your services. Market trends can provide context for your consulting offerings and help you anticipate future needs.

- **Trend Analysis:** Look for emerging trends in your target industries that could drive demand for your expertise. For example, the rise of digital transformation, an increased focus on sustainability, and advancements in technology could all create opportunities for consulting services.
- **Economic Factors:** Consider economic factors that may affect your target market, such as industry growth rates, regulatory changes, and shifts in consumer behaviour. Understanding these factors can help you anticipate changes in demand and adjust your strategy accordingly.

Step 5: Validate Your Findings. Validating your market research findings is an important step to ensure your conclusions are accurate and actionable. Validation can involve testing your assumptions with potential clients, seeking feedback from industry experts, or conducting a pilot project to gauge interest.

- **Pilot Projects:** Consider offering a limited pilot project or free consultation to a small group of potential clients. Use this opportunity to test your value proposition, gather feedback, and refine your approach based on real-world interactions.
- **Feedback Loops:** Establish feedback loops with clients, mentors, or colleagues to continuously refine your understanding of market demand. Regular feedback helps you stay attuned to client needs and adjust your services as necessary.

AI Reflection Prompt: *Here is what I know about my target market [insert details]. Can you suggest specific steps or tools to better understand the needs, trends, and pain points in this market?*

12.3 IDENTIFYING POTENTIAL CLIENTS AND INDUSTRIES

Identifying potential clients and industries is a critical part of your market research. Knowing who your ideal clients are and which industries are most likely to benefit from your services allows you to focus your marketing and outreach efforts effectively.

Tips for Identifying Potential Clients:

1. **Leverage Your Existing Network:** Start by tapping into your existing professional network. Reach out to former colleagues, industry contacts, or past clients who might benefit from your services or who can introduce you to potential leads.
2. **Use LinkedIn for Research:** LinkedIn is a powerful tool for identifying potential clients. Use LinkedIn's search features to find companies and individuals who fit your target market criteria. Look for decision-makers, such as CEOs, managers, or directors, who are likely to be interested in your services.
3. **Attend Industry Events:** Attending industry conferences, webinars, and networking events can help you connect with potential clients and learn more about their needs. Use these events to build relationships and gather insights into the challenges facing your target market.

4. **Explore Niche Marketplaces:** Depending on your niche, there may be specialised marketplaces or platforms where potential clients seek consultants. Explore platforms such as Upwork, Freelancer, or niche-specific sites that cater to your industry.

Tips for Exploring Relevant Industries:

1. **Research Industry Growth:** Focus on industries that are experiencing growth or transformation, as these are more likely to have a demand for consulting services. Look for sectors that align with your expertise and have a strong need for external support.
2. **Identify Key Players:** Identify the key players in your target industries, including companies that are leaders in their field or those undergoing significant change. These companies may have a greater need for consulting services to navigate challenges or capitalise on opportunities.
3. **Monitor Industry News:** Stay informed about the latest developments in your target industries by following industry news, subscribing to relevant newsletters, and joining industry associations. Being knowledgeable about current trends and challenges positions you as a valuable resource to potential clients.

AI Reflection Prompt: *Based on my background and expertise [insert your skills/experience], can you help me identify the types of clients and industries I should focus on for consulting opportunities?*

12.4 EVALUATING HOW YOUR SKILLS FIT THE MARKET

After conducting your market research, evaluate how your skills fit into the market landscape. This involves matching your expertise with the needs and pain points you have identified and determining how best to position your services.

Questions to Evaluate Fit:

1. **Do Your Skills Align with Market Needs?** Based on your research, assess whether your skills align with the identified needs of your target market. Are there specific areas where your expertise is in high demand? How well do your skills match the pain points and challenges faced by potential clients?

2. **Is There a Viable Market for Your Services?** Consider the size and viability of your target market. Are there enough potential clients who need your services to sustain your consulting business? Is the market growing, stable, or declining? Understanding market viability is crucial for long-term success.

3. **Can You Differentiate Yourself?** Evaluate your ability to differentiate yourself within the market. How does your unique value proposition compare to your competitors? Are there opportunities to carve out a unique niche or offer a distinctive approach that sets you apart?

AI Reflection Prompt: *Given these skills and experiences [insert your skills], how can I determine whether they align with current market needs and position myself effectively to meet those demands?*

12.5 ADAPTING YOUR STRATEGY BASED ON MARKET INSIGHTS

Market research is not a one-time activity; it is an ongoing process that informs your business strategy. Use the insights from your research to adapt and refine your consulting approach. This might involve tweaking your unique value proposition, targeting new client segments, adjusting your pricing, or expanding your service offerings.

Steps to Adapt Your Strategy:

1. **Refine Your UVP:** Based on market feedback, refine your UVP to better align with client needs and emphasise the aspects of your services that are most valuable to your target market.

2. **Adjust Your Marketing Efforts:** Use your research findings to adjust your marketing efforts, focusing on the channels and messages that resonate most with potential clients. Tailor your marketing materials to address the specific pain points and needs you have identified.

3. **Expand or Narrow Your Focus:** Depending on your market research, you may decide to expand your focus to include additional services or client segments. Conversely, you might narrow your focus to specialise in a specific niche where demand is strongest.

AI Reflection Prompt: *Here is what I've learned from my market research [insert insights]. Can you help me refine my consulting strategy, including my unique value proposition and target audience, based on these findings? [attach draft strategy]*

Understanding market demand for your expertise is a foundational step in building a successful consulting practice. By conducting thorough market research, identifying potential clients and industries, and evaluating how your skills fit into the market landscape, you can position yourself effectively and target the right opportunities.

Market research equips you with the knowledge needed to make strategic decisions about your consulting business, reducing risks and enhancing your chances of success. As you continue your journey into consulting, keep your finger on the pulse of the market, stay adaptable, and use your insights to guide your business growth and development.

KEY CONCEPTS

Market research is foundational to understanding demand for your consulting services. By analysing client needs, assessing competitors, and aligning your expertise with market trends, you can position yourself effectively and make informed, strategic decisions for a successful consulting business.

1. **Importance of Market Research**

Market research validates the demand for your services, helps you identify target clients, and informs strategic decisions such as pricing and marketing.

It reduces risks and increases your chances of success by providing insights into industry trends and client needs.

2. **Steps to Conduct Market Research**

Define Your Target Market: Identify industries, client sizes, and characteristics where your skills are most applicable.

Identify Needs and Pain Points: Understand client challenges through interviews, industry reports, and social media discussions.

Analyse Competitors: Assess competitors' offerings, pricing, strengths, and weaknesses to identify gaps you can fill.

Assess Market Trends: Stay informed about trends and economic factors that impact demand for your services.

Validate Findings: Test your assumptions with pilot projects, client feedback, and industry consultations.

3. **Identifying Potential Clients and Industries**

Use your network, LinkedIn, and industry events to identify potential clients and decision-makers.

Focus on industries experiencing growth or transformation to find clients with higher demand for consulting services.

4. Evaluating Market Fit for Your Skills

Match your expertise with the identified client needs and pain points.

Assess whether your services align with a viable, growing market.

Differentiate yourself with a unique value proposition or specialised expertise.

5. Adapting Your Strategy

Refine your unique value proposition based on market research and feedback.

Adjust marketing efforts to resonate with your target audience.

Expand or narrow your focus depending on where demand is strongest.

6. Using Market Insights

Incorporate research findings into your service offerings, messaging, and client targeting.

Continuously monitor and adapt to market shifts to stay relevant.

7. Ongoing Market Research

Treat market research as an ongoing process to anticipate client needs and remain competitive.

Use feedback loops to refine your understanding and adjust your business approach.

EXERCISE: MARKET DEMAND ASSESSMENT

Step 1: Identify Your Target Market. Clearly define your target market, including the industries, types of clients, and specific roles or decision-makers you aim to reach. Be as specific as possible to narrow your focus.

Step 2: Research Market Trends and Needs. Conduct research to understand the current trends, challenges, and needs within your target market. Use industry reports, surveys, articles, and conversations with industry professionals to gather insights.

Step 3: List Common Problems and Needs. From your research, list the common problems, needs, or gaps that your target clients are experiencing. Highlight those that align with your expertise and services.

Step 4: Validate Demand Through Direct Feedback. Reach out to potential clients, colleagues, or industry contacts to validate your findings. Ask about their biggest challenges and whether your proposed solutions resonate with them. *Example Questions for Validation:* What are the top three challenges your organisation is currently facing? How do you currently address these challenges? Would a solution like [your consulting service] be valuable to you?

Step 5: Reflect on Market Fit. Summarise your findings and consider how well your consulting services align with market demand. Are there adjustments or refinements needed to better meet your clients' needs?

Step 6: Action Plan. Based on your reflections, outline an action plan for further market validation or adjustments to your service offerings. This may include additional research, testing new service ideas, or refining your target audience.

13: NICHE SELECTION: FINDING THE RIGHT FIT

Selecting the right niche is one of the most important decisions you'll make as a consultant. A well-chosen niche allows you to focus your efforts, stand out in a crowded market, and position yourself as an expert in a specific area.

By aligning your strengths and expertise with market demand, you can attract clients who value your unique skills and are willing to pay a premium for your services.

In this chapter, we will explore strategies for selecting and validating a consulting niche that fits both market needs and your personal interests, ensuring a match between your strengths and demand.

13.1 THE IMPORTANCE OF NICHE SELECTION IN CONSULTING

Choosing a niche is about finding the sweet spot where your expertise, interests, and market demand intersect. A well-defined niche offers several benefits:

- **Differentiation:** It helps you stand out from generalist consultants by positioning you as a specialist in a specific area.

- **Targeted Marketing:** A niche allows you to tailor your marketing efforts to a specific audience, making your outreach more effective and resonant.
- **Higher Value and Pricing:** Clients are often willing to pay more for specialised expertise that directly addresses their needs.
- **Efficiency:** Working within a niche enables you to refine your processes, develop deep knowledge, and become more efficient in delivering your services.

The key to successful niche selection is ensuring that there is sufficient demand for your expertise and that the niche aligns with your personal interests and strengths.

This balance allows you to build a sustainable consulting practice that is both professionally rewarding and personally fulfilling.

> **AI Reflection Prompt:** *Based on my skills and experiences [insert your skills], how can I identify a niche that aligns with market demand and positions me as a specialist?*

13.2 STEPS TO SELECT AND VALIDATE YOUR NICHE

Selecting a niche involves both introspection and market analysis. By following a structured approach, you can identify a niche that aligns with your skills, passions, and market needs. Here are the key steps to guide you through the process:

Step 1: Reflect on Your Strengths and Interests

Start by reflecting on your own skills, experiences, and interests. Identifying what you are good at and what you enjoy doing is the foundation of effective niche selection.

- **Assess Your Skills and Expertise:** Make a list of your core skills, areas of expertise, and the types of problems you enjoy solving. Consider your past experiences, professional achievements, and feedback from colleagues or clients to identify where you excel.

- **Identify Your Passions:** Consider the aspects of your work that excite you most. Are there specific industries, challenges, or types of clients that you are particularly passionate about? Your enthusiasm for a particular area can be a powerful driver of success.

- **Consider Your Values and Motivations:** Reflect on your personal values and motivations. Are there causes or industries that resonate with your values? Aligning your niche with your personal values can add a deeper sense of purpose to your consulting work.

Step 2: Research Market Demand

Once you have a clear understanding of your strengths and interests, the next step is to research market demand. This involves identifying potential clients, understanding their needs, and evaluating the viability of your niche.

- **Identify Market Needs:** Use the market research techniques discussed in Chapter 12 to identify the specific needs and pain points of your target market. Look for areas where your skills can provide solutions to pressing challenges.

- **Evaluate Market Size and Viability:** Assess the size and viability of the potential market for your niche. Are there enough clients who need your services to sustain a consulting practice? Consider the market's growth potential and whether it aligns with your business goals.

- **Analyse Competitors:** Research other consultants or firms operating in your potential niche. Evaluate their service offerings, pricing, and positioning. Identify gaps in the market that you can fill or opportunities to differentiate yourself.

Step 3: Define Your Niche Criteria

To refine your niche selection, it's helpful to establish clear criteria that your niche must meet. This ensures that your chosen niche aligns with your business objectives and personal preferences.

Criteria to Consider:

- **Market Demand:** Is there sufficient demand for your services in this niche?
- **Alignment with Strengths:** Does the niche leverage your core skills and expertise?
- **Passion and Interest:** Are you genuinely interested in the niche and motivated to work in this area?
- **Profitability:** Can you charge rates that meet your financial goals in this niche?
- **Competition:** Is the market saturated, or is there room for a new player with your unique approach?

Prioritise Your Criteria: Rank your criteria in order of importance to help guide your decision-making. For example, if profitability is your top priority, you may prioritise niches with higher revenue potential, even if they are highly competitive.

Step 4: Test and Validate Your Niche

Before fully committing to a niche, it's important to test and validate your choice. This allows you to gather feedback, assess client interest, and make adjustments as needed.

- **Conduct Pilot Projects:** Offer your services on a small scale to a few select clients within your chosen niche. Use these pilot projects to test your value proposition, refine your service offerings, and gauge client satisfaction.
- **Seek Feedback:** Actively seek feedback from your pilot clients, industry contacts, or mentors. Ask them about their experience working with you, what they found valuable, and any areas for improvement.
- **Adjust Based on Feedback:** Use the feedback you receive to refine your niche and service offerings. Be open to making

adjustments based on client needs, market conditions, or new insights you gain during the validation process.

Step 5: Commit to Your Niche and Position Yourself as an Expert

Once you have validated your niche, it's time to fully commit and position yourself as an expert in that area. Specialising in a niche requires a strategic approach to marketing, branding, and client engagement.

Develop Niche-Specific Marketing Materials: Create marketing materials, such as your website, LinkedIn profile, and promotional content, that clearly communicate your niche and the value you provide. Highlight your expertise, past successes, and how you solve specific problems for your target clients.

Engage with Your Niche Community: Build your presence in your niche community by participating in industry events, joining relevant associations, or contributing to niche-specific publications. Networking within your niche helps you establish credibility and connect with potential clients.

Create Niche-Focused Content: Position yourself as a thought leader by creating content that addresses the needs and challenges of your niche. This could include blog posts, webinars, white papers, or case studies that showcase your expertise and provide value to your target audience.

> **AI Reflection Prompts:** *Here are my strengths, interests, and values [insert details]. Can you help me identify potential niches that align with these factors?*
>
> *Using this market research data [insert findings], how can I assess whether my chosen niche has sufficient demand and profitability?*
>
> *What are some practical ways to test and validate my niche idea before fully committing to it?*

13.3 STRATEGIES FOR FINDING THE RIGHT NICHE FIT

Finding the right niche fit involves balancing your personal interests with market demand. Here are some additional strategies to help you select a niche that aligns with both:

1. **Start Broad and Narrow Down:** If you're struggling to choose a niche, start with a broader focus and gradually narrow it down based on your experiences and market feedback.
2. **Leverage Your Existing Network:** Your existing network can be a valuable resource for identifying potential niches. Reach out to former colleagues, clients, or industry contacts to explore areas where your expertise could be in demand. Networking conversations can often reveal niche opportunities you had not considered.
3. **Look for Underserved Markets:** Identify underserved markets or niche segments that are not being fully addressed by current consultants. These could be emerging industries, specific technologies, or unique client demographics. Underserved markets often present opportunities for differentiation and growth.
4. **Consider the Long-Term Viability:** When selecting a niche, think about its long-term viability. Is the niche growing, or is it likely to decline over time? Consider how your niche aligns with broader industry trends and whether it offers potential for sustained demand and career growth.
5. **Align with Your Personal Brand:** Ensure that your niche aligns with your personal brand and the image you want to project as a consultant. Your niche should reflect your professional identity, values, and the type of work you want to be known for. A strong personal brand can enhance your visibility and credibility within your niche.

AI Reflection Prompts: *I'm considering these potential niches [insert options]. Can you help me narrow them down based on long-term viability and market trends?*

What steps can I take to leverage my professional network to uncover potential niche opportunities?

How can I identify underserved markets or emerging industries that align with my expertise?

13.4 COMMON PITFALLS TO AVOID IN NICHE SELECTION

While niche selection offers many benefits, there are common pitfalls that can hinder your success. Being aware of these pitfalls can help you make a more informed decision:

1. **Choosing a Niche Based Solely on Interest:** While personal interest is important, it is not enough on its own. Ensure that there is a viable market demand for your chosen niche. A niche based solely on interest without considering market needs may struggle to generate sufficient business.
2. **Targeting Too Broad a Market:** Avoid the temptation to cast a wide net in an attempt to appeal to more clients. A broad focus can dilute your messaging and make it harder to stand out. A narrower, well-defined niche allows you to deliver more targeted and effective solutions.
3. **Ignoring Market Research:** Failing to conduct thorough market research can lead to choosing a niche with limited demand or high competition. Make sure to base your decision on data and insights rather than assumptions or anecdotal evidence.
4. **Overcommitting Before Validation:** Committing fully to a niche without first testing and validating it can be risky. Pilot projects and feedback loops are essential to ensuring that your chosen niche is the right fit before making significant investments in marketing or branding.

Selecting the right niche is a strategic decision that lays the foundation for your consulting business. By aligning your skills, interests, and market demand, you can identify a niche that offers both professional fulfilment and business success. The process of niche selection involves introspection, market research, and validation, but the effort pays off by positioning you as a specialist who delivers targeted value to your clients.

As you move forward, continue to refine your niche based on market feedback and evolving trends. A well-chosen niche not only differentiates you in the consulting market but also creates a clear path for growth, client engagement, and long-term success.

> **AI Reflection Prompts:** *How can I ensure that I don't choose a niche based solely on personal interest without validating market demand?*
>
> *I'm concerned about targeting too broad a market. Can you help me define a more specific focus within my niche?*
>
> *What tools or methods can I use to avoid making assumptions and instead base my niche selection on solid market research?*

KEY CONCEPTS

Selecting the right niche requires balancing your strengths, passions, and market demand. A defined niche allows you to specialise, attract high-value clients, and build credibility. By researching, testing, and refining your niche, you can establish a consulting practice that aligns with your expertise and delivers meaningful results.

1. Importance of Niche Selection

A well-chosen niche helps you stand out as a specialist, enables targeted marketing, and attracts clients willing to pay a premium for expertise.

Aligning your strengths and interests with market demand creates a sustainable and fulfilling consulting practice.

2. Steps to Select and Validate Your Niche

Reflect on Strengths and Interests: Identify your core skills, passions, and values to narrow your focus.

Research Market Demand: Use tools like client interviews, industry reports, and competitor analysis to ensure there is sufficient demand.

Define Niche Criteria: Assess factors such as market size, profitability, alignment with your expertise, and personal interest.

Test and Validate: Pilot your services, gather feedback, and refine your offerings before fully committing.

Commit and Position Yourself: Once validated, create niche-specific marketing materials, engage with your niche community, and build authority through content.

3. Strategies for Finding the Right Niche Fit

Start broad and narrow down based on feedback and experience.

Leverage your network for insights and opportunities.

Target underserved markets or emerging industries.

Consider long-term viability by aligning your niche with industry trends.

Align your niche with your personal brand to enhance credibility and visibility.

4. Common Pitfalls to Avoid

Choosing a niche based only on personal interest without validating market demand.

Targeting too broad a market, which dilutes your messaging and appeal.

Ignoring market research, leading to misaligned choices.

Overcommitting to a niche without testing and validating its potential.

5. Niche Evaluation Framework

Use a matrix to evaluate potential niches against criteria such as market demand, income potential, and alignment with skills.

Score and analyse niches to identify the best fit for your consulting business.

6. Ongoing Refinement

Continuously refine your niche based on market feedback and evolving trends.

A well-chosen niche positions you as a trusted expert and paves the way for growth and long-term success.

EXERCISE: NICHE EVALUATION MATRIX

Step 1: List Potential Niches. Based on your skills, market research, and personal interests, list the top 3-5 potential niches you are considering for your consulting practice.

Step 2: Define Evaluation Criteria. Identify key criteria for evaluating these niches. Consider factors such as:

- Alignment with your expertise
- Market demand and growth potential
- Competition and saturation
- Personal interest and passion
- Income potential
- Client accessibility

Step 3: Create a Niche Evaluation Matrix. Create a matrix with your potential niches listed in rows and your evaluation criteria listed in columns. Rate each niche against each criterion on a scale of 1 (low) to 5 (high).

Step 4: Analyse Your Results. Review your ratings and identify which niche scores the highest overall. Consider whether this niche aligns well with your goals and values.

Step 5: Reflect on Your Niche Choice. Reflect on your top-scoring niche. How excited do you feel about pursuing this niche? Does it align with your vision for your consulting practice? Are there any additional steps you need to take to validate or refine your choice?

Step 6: Next Steps. Outline the next steps you need to take to establish yourself in your chosen niche, such as further market research, building specific skills, or developing targeted marketing strategies.

14: TESTING THE WATERS: EXPLORING CONSULTING PART-TIME

Transitioning into consulting full-time can feel like a daunting leap, especially if you are unsure whether consulting is the right fit for you or if you are not ready to give up the security of your current job.

Exploring consulting on a part-time basis or through small projects allows you to gain experience, test your skills, and build confidence without the immediate pressure of a full-time commitment.

In this chapter, we discuss strategies for experimenting with consulting part-time, offering a low-risk approach to gaining experience while maintaining your current employment.

14.1 THE BENEFITS OF PART-TIME CONSULTING

Part-time consulting offers several advantages for those considering a shift into this field:

Low-Risk Exploration: By consulting part-time, you can explore the field without the financial risks associated with leaving a full-time job. This approach allows you to test your consulting skills and assess market demand while keeping your primary source of income intact.

Skill Development: Part-time consulting provides an opportunity to develop and refine your consulting skills, such as client management, project delivery, and business development, in a real-world setting.

Building a Portfolio: Working on smaller projects enables you to create a portfolio of consulting work, including case studies, testimonials, and references, which can be invaluable if you decide to transition to full-time consulting in the future.

Networking and Exposure: Part-time consulting helps you expand your professional network and gain exposure to different industries and clients. This network can serve as a foundation for future consulting opportunities.

> **AI Reflection Prompt:** *What do I need to consider if I use part-time consulting to test my consulting skills and market demand while maintaining the financial security of my full-time job?*

14.2 STRATEGIES FOR PART-TIME CONSULTING

Exploring consulting part-time requires careful planning and strategic effort. Here are some strategies to help you get started:

1. Offer Consulting Services to Your Current Employer

One of the easiest ways to start consulting part-time is by offering your services to your current employer in a consulting capacity. If your current role involves expertise that could be outsourced, discuss the possibility of taking on consulting projects outside your standard job responsibilities.

Identify Gaps or Needs: Look for areas within your organisation where your skills could provide additional value. This could involve taking on special projects, providing strategic advice, or offering support during periods of high demand.

Propose a Consulting Arrangement: Approach your employer with a clear proposal outlining the scope of the consulting work, the benefits to the organisation, and how it can be managed alongside your existing responsibilities. Be prepared to discuss how you will maintain boundaries between your full-time role and consulting work.

2. Leverage Your Network for Part-Time Opportunities

Your professional network is a valuable resource for finding part-time consulting opportunities. Reach out to former colleagues, clients, or industry contacts to inform them that you are available for consulting on a limited basis.

Use LinkedIn and Professional Groups: Update your LinkedIn profile to reflect your availability for part-time consulting and actively engage in professional groups where potential clients may be seeking your expertise. Share content or insights that demonstrate your knowledge and enhance your visibility.

Attend Networking Events: Attend industry conferences, meetups, or webinars to connect with potential clients. Networking events provide a platform to introduce your consulting services and explore small project opportunities.

3. Start with Freelance Platforms and Job Boards

Freelance platforms like Upwork, Freelancer, and Fiverr offer a range of project-based consulting opportunities that can be completed part-time. These platforms allow you to browse available projects, submit proposals, and build a portfolio of consulting work.

Optimise Your Profile: Create a detailed profile highlighting your skills, experience, and the specific consulting services you offer. Use keywords that reflect your niche to make your profile discoverable by potential clients.

Select Small, Manageable Projects: Start with smaller projects that align with your expertise and can be completed within your available time. This approach allows you to gain experience without overcommitting.

4. Offer Pro Bono or Discounted Services to Gain Experience

Offering pro bono or discounted consulting services can be a strategic way to gain initial experience and build a client base. Consider reaching out to non-profits, small businesses, or startups that could benefit from your expertise but may not have the budget for full-priced consulting services.

Select Clients Strategically: Choose pro bono or discounted projects that are relevant to your niche and can provide valuable case studies or testimonials. Ensure that the terms of your arrangement are clear and that the client understands the value of your work, even if it's provided at a reduced rate.

Use Pro Bono Work as a Marketing Tool: Pro bono projects can serve as a marketing tool, showcasing your capabilities and helping you establish a reputation in your target market. Use the results of these projects to build credibility and attract paying clients.

5. Develop a Side Business Plan for Consulting

If you're serious about exploring part-time consulting, consider developing a side business plan that outlines your goals, target market, and strategies for acquiring clients. A side business plan helps you approach part-time consulting with a strategic mindset, ensuring that your efforts are focused and purposeful.

Define Your Services and Target Market: Clearly define the consulting services you will offer and identify your target market. Understanding whom you want to serve and how you can provide value is critical for successful part-time consulting.

Set Goals and Metrics: Establish specific goals for your part-time consulting, such as the number of projects you want to complete, income targets, or skills you aim to develop. Set metrics to track your progress and adjust your approach as needed.

AI Reflection Prompt: *What are the best strategies for me to find part-time consulting opportunities, such as leveraging my current employer, network, or freelance platforms, based on my expertise [insert your expertise]?*

14.3 BALANCING PART-TIME CONSULTING WITH FULL-TIME EMPLOYMENT

Balancing part-time consulting with your full-time job requires careful time management and clear boundaries. Here are some tips to help you manage both commitments effectively:

1. Manage Your Time Wisely

Effective time management is essential for balancing part-time consulting with full-time employment. Use tools such as calendars, task lists, and project management software to organise your time and ensure that you can meet both your consulting and job responsibilities.

Set Specific Work Hours for Consulting: Designate specific hours for consulting work, such as evenings, weekends, or designated days off. Sticking to a set schedule helps you maintain consistency and prevents consulting work from encroaching on your full-time job.

Prioritise Tasks and Avoid Overcommitment: Prioritise your consulting tasks based on deadlines, client needs, and their impact on your business goals. Be mindful of your capacity and avoid overcommitting to projects that could interfere with your full-time job.

2. Maintain Professional Boundaries

Maintaining professional boundaries between your consulting work and full-time job is crucial for managing both effectively and ethically. Be transparent with your employer if there is any potential overlap, and ensure that your consulting activities do not conflict with your job responsibilities.

Separate Workspaces: If possible, create separate workspaces for your consulting and full-time job. This helps establish a physical distinction between the two roles and reinforces boundaries.

Respect Employer Policies: Be aware of any company policies regarding outside work or conflicts of interest. If necessary, seek permission from your employer to engage in consulting activities outside of your full-time role.

3. Use Part-Time Consulting as a Learning Opportunity

Approach part-time consulting as a learning opportunity to refine your skills, test your market fit, and gain insights into the consulting world. Use this time to experiment with different services, pricing models, and client engagement strategies.

Reflect on Your Experiences: Regularly reflect on your consulting experiences to identify what is working well and where improvements are needed. Use this feedback to adjust your approach and develop best practices for future consulting engagements.

Build Your Confidence: Part-time consulting allows you to build confidence in your consulting abilities without the full pressure of a complete career change. Celebrate your successes, learn from challenges, and gradually cultivate the confidence necessary to pursue consulting full-time, if desired.

> **AI Reflection Prompt:** *What time management and boundary-setting techniques can I use to balance part-time consulting with my current full-time job effectively and ethically?*

14.4 RECOGNISING WHEN YOU'RE READY TO TRANSITION

Part-time consulting provides a valuable testing ground, but there may come a point when you are ready to transition to consulting full-time.

Recognising when you are ready involves assessing your financial stability, market demand, and personal readiness for a full-time consulting career.

Indicators That You're Ready to Transition:

1. **Consistent Demand for Your Services:** If you are consistently attracting clients and have a steady pipeline of consulting work, this indicates a strong market demand for your services. Consistent demand can provide the financial stability needed to transition full-time.
2. **Financial Readiness:** Evaluate your financial readiness to make the transition, including having a sufficient financial buffer, manageable expenses, and a realistic income projection from consulting. Financial readiness is a key factor in reducing the stress of transitioning to full-time consulting.
3. **Desire for Greater Control and Flexibility:** If you find that you enjoy the autonomy and variety of consulting more than your full-time job, it may be a sign that you are ready to make the shift. Consulting offers the opportunity to shape your career and lifestyle on your terms.
4. **Confidence in Your Consulting Skills:** Confidence in your consulting skills and business acumen is crucial for making a successful transition. If your part-time consulting experiences have strengthened your skills and provided valuable insights, you may be ready to take the next step.

   AI Reflection Prompt: *Based on the indicators of readiness (consistent client demand, financial stability, and confidence), how can I evaluate if I am ready to transition from part-time to full-time consulting?*

Exploring part-time consulting offers a low-risk way to gain experience, build confidence, and validate your readiness for a full-time consulting career. By leveraging your existing network, taking on small projects, and strategically managing your time, you can test the waters of consulting while maintaining the security of your current employment.

As you gain experience and refine your consulting approach, you will be better equipped to make an informed decision about whether consulting is the right path for you. Whether you choose to continue consulting part-time, transition to full-time, or simply use the experience to enhance your current career, part-time consulting provides valuable lessons and opportunities for professional growth.

KEY CONCEPTS

Part-time consulting is a low-risk way to explore the field, build experience, and validate your readiness for full-time consulting. It offers valuable insights while maintaining the security of your current employment.

1. Benefits of Part-Time Consulting

Allows you to explore consulting without financial risks or leaving your full-time job.

Provides real-world opportunities to refine consulting skills such as client management and project delivery.

Helps build a portfolio of case studies, testimonials, and references for future full-time consulting.

Expands your professional network and exposes you to new industries and clients.

2. Strategies for Part-Time Consulting

Offer Services to Your Current Employer: Propose consulting arrangements to address organisational needs or gaps.

Leverage Your Network: Use LinkedIn, professional groups, and networking events to find small projects.

Use Freelance Platforms: Platforms like Upwork or Fiverr provide low-commitment, project-based opportunities.

Offer Pro Bono Work: Gain experience and build credibility by strategically selecting clients for discounted or free services.

Develop a Side Business Plan: Define goals, target markets, and services to approach consulting part-time with focus.

3. Balancing Part-Time Consulting with Full-Time Employment

Manage time effectively with tools like calendars and task lists, and set specific hours for consulting.

Maintain clear professional boundaries between your full-time job and consulting projects.

Use part-time consulting as a learning opportunity to test services, pricing models, and client engagement strategies.

4. Recognising When You're Ready to Transition

Indicators include consistent client demand, financial readiness (including buffer and income projections), and confidence in your consulting abilities.

A desire for autonomy and control may signal readiness for a full-time consulting career.

5. Designing a Part-Time Consulting Pilot

Define small-scale projects with manageable scope and clear objectives to test your skills and market fit.

Set boundaries for time commitments and deliverables to ensure balance with your current job.

Reflect on experiences to identify lessons learned and refine your approach.

EXERCISE: DESIGNING A PART-TIME CONSULTING PILOT

Step 1: Define Your Pilot Project. Identify a small-scale consulting project or client engagement that you can pursue part-time. Consider offering a limited scope of your services or working with a familiar client or in a familiar industry.

Step 2: Set Clear Objectives. Outline the objectives of your pilot project. What do you hope to learn or achieve from this experience? Objectives might include testing your consulting skills, gaining client feedback, or understanding workload management.

Step 3: Establish Boundaries and Time Commitments. Define the boundaries for your part-time consulting, such as specific working hours, limits on project scope, and clear deliverables. Ensure that these commitments are manageable alongside your current job or other responsibilities.

Step 4: Develop a Mini-Plan. Create a mini-plan for your pilot, including key steps, timelines, and resources needed. Outline how you will find your first client, deliver your services, and measure success.

Step 5: Reflect on Your Experience. After completing your pilot project, take time to reflect on the experience. What went well, and what challenges did you encounter? How did consulting part-time fit with your current lifestyle and commitments?

Step 6: Make Adjustments. Based on your reflections, identify any adjustments needed if you decide to continue consulting part-time or scale up to full-time consulting. Use these insights to refine your approach and improve your readiness.

15: PIVOTING YOUR NICHE: STAYING ADAPTABLE

I n the consulting world, change is constant. Market demands shift, industries evolve, and your professional interests may develop over time.

While selecting a niche is a crucial step in building your consulting business, the ability to pivot or refine your focus is equally important. Being adaptable allows you to respond to market feedback, seize new opportunities, and align your consulting practice with your evolving skills and interests.

In this chapter, we explore the importance of flexibility in niche selection and provide practical advice on how to pivot or refine your focus when needed.

15.1 THE NEED FOR ADAPTABILITY IN CONSULTING

Adaptability is a key trait for successful consultants. The business landscape is dynamic, and what works today may not work tomorrow. A niche that once had high demand can become oversaturated or less relevant as industries change. Likewise, your professional interests may shift, leading you to explore new areas where you can apply your expertise.

By staying adaptable, you can ensure that your consulting practice remains relevant, resilient, and aligned with both market needs and your personal goals.

Why Adaptability Matters:

- **Responding to Market Changes:** Market conditions can change rapidly due to technological advancements, regulatory shifts, or economic fluctuations. Being adaptable allows you to pivot your niche to meet new demands and stay competitive.
- **Seizing Emerging Opportunities:** New opportunities often arise in unexpected places. By remaining flexible, you can quickly adjust your focus to capitalise on emerging trends or untapped markets.
- **Aligning with Evolving Interests:** Over time, your professional interests and strengths may evolve. An adaptable mindset allows you to refine your niche in a way that keeps your work fulfilling and aligned with your passions.

AI Reflection Prompt: Given that market demands and my professional interests [insert interests] may evolve, how can I ensure my consulting practice remains adaptable and aligned with emerging opportunities?

15.2 RECOGNISING WHEN IT'S TIME TO PIVOT

Pivoting your niche is not a sign of failure; rather, it is a strategic decision to better align your consulting business with the current market landscape or your personal goals. Recognising when it's time to pivot involves being attuned to both external market signals and internal indicators.

Signs It May Be Time to Pivot Your Niche:

1. **Declining Demand or Saturation:** If you notice a decline in demand for your services or an increase in competition that

makes it difficult to stand out, it may be time to explore alternative niches with greater potential for growth.

2. **Client Feedback and Market Insights:** Pay attention to feedback from clients and insights gained through market research. If clients consistently request services outside your current niche or if market trends indicate new areas of need, these are valuable signals that a pivot could be beneficial.

3. **Misalignment with Your Strengths:** If you find that your current niche no longer aligns with your core strengths or that you are not fully leveraging your expertise, consider refining your focus to better match your skills.

4. **Evolving Professional Interests:** As you gain experience, your interests and motivations may evolve. If you are feeling unfulfilled or disengaged with your current niche, it may be time to pivot to an area that excites and energises you.

5. **Financial Considerations:** If your current niche is not meeting your financial goals or if profitability is declining, exploring a different niche with higher revenue potential may be a necessary step to sustain your consulting business.

AI Reflection Prompt: *What signals, such as declining demand or misalignment with my strengths, should I monitor to determine whether it is time to pivot my consulting niche?*

15.3 STEPS TO PIVOT OR REFINE YOUR NICHE

Pivoting or refining your niche requires careful consideration and strategic planning. Here are steps to guide you through the process of making a successful pivot:

Step 1: Reassess Your Skills and Interests

Begin by reassessing your skills, expertise, and interests to identify areas where you can provide the most value. Reflect on your recent experiences, successes, and any feedback you have received that might point to a new direction.

Conduct a Skills Inventory: List your current skills, including any new competencies you have developed. Consider how these skills can be applied in different contexts or industries.

Identify Emerging Interests: Reflect on your recent projects or professional experiences to identify areas that have sparked your interest. Are there new challenges or opportunities that excite you? Use this reflection to explore potential new niches.

Step 2: Research New Market Opportunities

Once you have a clearer understanding of your skills and interests, research new market opportunities where your expertise could be valuable. Look for trends, emerging industries, or niche areas that align with your strengths and have growing demand.

Explore Industry Trends: Use industry reports, publications, and online resources to identify emerging trends that are driving demand for consulting services. Consider how your skills can be adapted to meet these new needs.

Evaluate Market Viability: Assess the viability of potential niches by evaluating factors such as market size, client demand, and competition. Look for niches that offer a balance of sufficient demand and room for differentiation.

Step 3: Test Your New Niche on a Small Scale

Before fully committing to a new niche, test your pivot on a small scale. This approach allows you to validate your ideas, gather feedback, and make adjustments without the risk of a full-scale shift.

Offer a Pilot Service: Develop a pilot version of your new service offering and introduce it to a select group of clients. Use this pilot phase to refine your approach, validate your value proposition, and assess client interest.

Seek Feedback: Actively seek feedback from your pilot clients to understand what works well and where improvements are needed. Use this feedback to make data-driven decisions about whether to proceed with the pivot or refine your approach further.

Step 4: Update Your Marketing and Positioning

If you decide to move forward with the pivot, update your marketing and positioning to reflect your new niche. Clearly communicate the change to your existing clients, network, and target audience.

Revise Your UVP: Update your unique value proposition to align with your new niche. Ensure that it clearly communicates the specific value you offer and how you address the needs of your new target market.

Refresh Your Marketing Materials: Update your website, LinkedIn profile, and other marketing materials to reflect your new niche and services. Highlight your relevant expertise and any early successes or case studies from your pilot projects.

Leverage Content Marketing: Use content marketing to build credibility in your new niche. Share insights,

thought leadership, and success stories that demonstrate your expertise and value to potential clients.

Step 5: Monitor and Adapt Continuously

A successful pivot is not a one-time event but an ongoing process of monitoring, learning, and adapting. Continuously assess your performance, gather client feedback, and stay attuned to market trends to ensure that your consulting practice remains aligned with evolving needs.

Set Metrics and Track Progress: Establish key metrics to track the success of your pivot, such as client acquisition, revenue growth, or client satisfaction. Regularly review these metrics to gauge the effectiveness of your new niche and make adjustments as needed.

Stay Open to Further Refinement: Be open to refining your niche as you gain more insights and experience. Flexibility is key to staying relevant and competitive in the consulting market.

> **AI Reflection Prompt:** *If I were to pivot my niche, can you help me outline a plan to reassess my skills, research new market opportunities, and test potential niches on a small scale?*

15.4 EMBRACING A MINDSET OF CONTINUOUS LEARNING AND ADAPTATION

A successful consulting career is built on a foundation of continuous learning and adaptation. Embracing a mindset of growth and flexibility allows you to navigate changes in the market, pivot when necessary, and evolve your consulting practice over time.

Key Strategies for Maintaining Adaptability:

1. **Commit to Lifelong Learning:** Stay current with industry trends, emerging technologies, and new methodologies by committing to lifelong learning. This could involve taking courses, attending conferences, or participating in professional communities.

2. **Cultivate a Growth Mindset:** A growth mindset—the belief that your abilities and intelligence can be developed through effort and learning—enables you to view challenges as opportunities for growth. Cultivating this mindset will help you remain resilient and open to change.

3. **Be Proactive in Seeking Feedback:** Regularly seek feedback from clients, peers, and mentors to gain insights into how you can improve and adapt your services. Feedback is a valuable tool for identifying areas for refinement and staying aligned with client needs.

4. **Stay Connected to Your Network:** Maintain strong connections within your professional network to stay informed about industry developments and potential collaboration opportunities. Your network can also provide valuable support and advice as you navigate changes in your consulting business.

AI Reflection Prompt: *What strategies can I adopt to stay current with industry trends and cultivate a mindset of continuous learning to remain flexible and resilient as a consultant?*

15.5 COMMON CHALLENGES IN PIVOTING AND HOW TO OVERCOME THEM

Pivoting your niche can present challenges, but with the right approach, these challenges can be effectively managed. Here are some common challenges and strategies for overcoming them:

1. **Fear of Letting Go of Your Current Niche:** Letting go of an established niche can be difficult, especially if you've invested significant time and effort. To overcome this, focus on the potential benefits of the pivot and how it aligns with your long-term goals.
2. **Uncertainty About Market Fit:** It's normal to feel uncertain about whether a new niche will be successful. Mitigate this risk by testing your pivot on a small scale and using data and feedback to guide your decisions.
3. **Resistance to Change:** Change can be uncomfortable, but it's essential for growth. Embrace change as a necessary part of staying relevant and competitive. Set small, manageable goals to build momentum and confidence in your pivot.
4. **Maintaining Consistency During the Transition:** Pivoting your niche while maintaining consistency in your client service and business operations can be challenging. Plan your transition carefully, communicate clearly with clients, and ensure that your core values and quality standards remain consistent.

Staying adaptable and open to pivoting your niche is a vital aspect of a successful consulting career. By recognising when it's time to pivot, strategically testing new niches, and embracing a mindset of continuous learning and flexibility, you can navigate changes in the market and align your consulting practice with evolving needs and opportunities.

Pivoting is not a sign of failure but a proactive response to change. It's about positioning yourself to thrive in a dynamic environment and ensuring that your consulting business remains relevant, resilient, and fulfilling. As you continue your consulting journey, remember that adaptability is one of your greatest strengths—use it to stay ahead of the curve and create a consulting practice that grows with you.

> **AI Reflection Prompt:** *How can I overcome common challenges like the fear of letting go of my current niche or uncertainty about market fit when considering a pivot in my consulting practice?*

KEY CONCEPTS

Pivoting is a proactive strategy, not a sign of failure. It allows consultants to align their practices with changing market needs, seize opportunities, and maintain relevance and growth.

1. The Need for Adaptability in Consulting

Adaptability ensures your consulting practice remains relevant in dynamic markets.

It helps you respond to market changes, seize emerging opportunities, and align with evolving professional interests.

2. Recognising When It's Time to Pivot

Declining demand or oversaturation in your current niche.

Client feedback and market insights pointing to untapped opportunities.

Misalignment with your strengths or evolving professional interests.

Financial challenges requiring a shift to a more profitable niche.

3. Steps to Pivot or Refine Your Niche

Reassess Your Skills and Interests: Inventory your skills and reflect on recent successes to explore new directions.

Research Market Opportunities: Identify trends, emerging industries, and niche areas with growth potential.

Test Your New Niche: Pilot small-scale projects to validate demand and refine your offerings.

Update Marketing and Positioning: Revise your UVP, marketing materials, and messaging to reflect the new focus.

Monitor and Adapt: Track metrics like client acquisition and revenue to gauge success and make further refinements.

4. Embracing Continuous Learning and Adaptation

Commit to lifelong learning to stay current with industry trends and methodologies.

Cultivate a growth mindset to view challenges as opportunities for development.

Build strong professional networks for insights, collaboration, and feedback.

5. Common Challenges in Pivoting and How to Overcome Them

Fear of Letting Go: Focus on the benefits of change and alignment with long-term goals.

Market Uncertainty: Mitigate risk by testing new niches on a small scale.

Resistance to Change: Set manageable goals to ease into the transition.

Maintaining Consistency: Communicate clearly with clients and ensure that service quality remains consistent during the pivot.

EXERCISE: PIVOT READINESS PLAN

Step 1: Identify Pivot Triggers. List potential triggers that might signal a need to pivot your niche, such as changes in market demand, increased competition, or misalignment with your interests or skills.

Step 2: Assess Your Flexibility. Reflect on your willingness to adapt and pivot your niche if necessary. Consider past experiences in which you successfully adapted to change and how those skills can be applied to consulting.

Step 3: Develop Pivot Scenarios. Create a few "what-if" scenarios that involve pivoting your niche. For each scenario, outline possible steps you would take to adjust your services, target a new audience, or reposition your consulting business.

Step 4: Set Up a Feedback Loop. Establish a feedback loop to continuously assess the effectiveness of your current niche. This could include regular check-ins with clients, tracking industry trends, or reviewing your own satisfaction and performance.

Step 5: Reflect on Your Adaptability. Write a brief reflection on your adaptability and comfort with pivoting. How prepared do you feel to make changes if your current niche isn't working? What resources or support would help you make a successful pivot?

Step 6: Plan for Flexibility. Outline specific actions you can take to build flexibility into your consulting business, such as diversifying your service offerings, staying updated on market trends, or maintaining a broad network that allows for easy shifts.

PART 4: DECISION-MAKING: IS SOLO CONSULTING RIGHT FOR YOU?

Twenty years from now you will be more disappointed by the things that you didn't do than by the ones you did do. So throw off the bowlines. Sail away from the safe harbor. Catch the trade winds in your sails. Explore. Dream. Discover.

MARK TWAIN

16: WEIGHING THE PROS AND CONS FOR YOUR SITUATION

Deciding whether to transition into solo consulting is a deeply personal choice that depends on your unique circumstances, goals, and values.

While consulting offers significant benefits, such as autonomy, flexibility, and the potential for higher earnings, it also comes with challenges, including income variability, financial risk, and the demands of self-management.

This chapter will provide a framework to help you evaluate the personal and professional pros and cons of consulting based on your individual situation, guiding you towards a balanced and informed decision.

16.1 UNDERSTANDING THE KEY FACTORS IN YOUR DECISION

Before diving into the pros and cons of consulting, it's important to consider the key factors that will influence your decision. These factors may include your financial situation, career goals, risk tolerance, lifestyle preferences, and personal values. By clarifying these factors, you can create a personalised framework for evaluating whether consulting aligns with your overall vision for your career and life.

Key Factors to Consider:

- **Financial Readiness:** Assess your current financial stability, savings, and income needs. Are you in a position where you can manage the financial uncertainties of consulting?
- **Career Goals:** Reflect on your long-term career goals. Does consulting provide a path that aligns with your aspirations for growth, impact, and fulfilment?
- **Risk Tolerance:** Consider your comfort level with risk, including income variability and the entrepreneurial aspects of consulting. Are you willing and able to embrace the uncertainties that come with self-employment?
- **Work-Life Balance:** Evaluate your lifestyle preferences and priorities. Does consulting offer the flexibility and control you need to achieve your desired work-life balance?
- **Personal Values:** Think about your core values and how they align with consulting. Do you value independence, creativity, and the ability to shape your own work, or do you prefer the stability and structure of traditional employment?

AI Reflection Prompt: *Based on my financial readiness, career goals, risk tolerance, and lifestyle preferences [insert details], how can I assess whether solo consulting aligns with my long-term vision?*

16.2 THE PROFESSIONAL PROS AND CONS OF SOLO CONSULTING

Solo consulting offers a range of professional benefits, but it also comes with challenges. Evaluating these pros and cons in the context of your career can help you determine whether consulting is a suitable path.

Professional Pros of Solo Consulting:

1. **Autonomy and Control:** As a solo consultant, you have the freedom to choose your projects, clients, and working hours.

This autonomy allows you to shape your career according to your preferences and priorities, providing a level of control that is often not possible in traditional employment.

2. **Diverse Project Opportunities:** Consulting offers the chance to work on a variety of projects across different industries and clients. This diversity can be intellectually stimulating and provides opportunities for continuous learning and professional growth.

3. **Potential for Higher Earnings:** Depending on your niche and expertise, consulting can offer the potential for higher earnings compared to a salaried position. Consultants can command premium rates for specialised skills, and with effective business management, the income potential can be significant.

4. **Opportunity for Thought Leadership:** Consulting allows you to position yourself as a thought leader in your field. Through content creation, speaking engagements, and strategic networking, you can build a strong personal brand and establish yourself as an expert.

5. **Flexibility in Work-Life Balance:** The flexibility of consulting can provide a better work-life balance, allowing you to set your own schedule and work environment. This can be especially beneficial for those with family commitments or personal pursuits outside of work.

Professional Cons of Solo Consulting:

1. **Income Variability and Financial Risk:** One of the biggest challenges of consulting is the variability of income. Unlike a regular paycheck, consulting income can fluctuate based on client demand, project timelines, and market conditions. This financial uncertainty requires careful planning and management.

2. **Responsibility for Business Operations:** As a solo consultant, you are responsible for all aspects of your business, including marketing, sales, finance, and administration. This can be time-

consuming and requires skills beyond your core consulting expertise.

3. **Isolation and Lack of Team Dynamics:** Consulting can be isolating, especially if you're used to working in a team environment. The lack of daily interaction with colleagues can be a significant adjustment, and consultants must proactively seek out networking opportunities to stay connected.

4. **Pressure to Consistently Find Clients:** Business development is a continuous effort in consulting. The pressure to consistently find and secure clients can be stressful, especially during slow periods. Consultants must be proactive in networking, marketing, and maintaining a steady pipeline of work.

5. **Limited Benefits and Security:** Consulting does not come with the benefits and security of traditional employment, such as health insurance, retirement plans, or paid leave. Consultants must manage and fund their own benefits, which can add to the financial burden.

> **AI Reflection Prompt:** *Given my professional skills and ambitions [insert skills/goals], can you help me weigh the key advantages and challenges of solo consulting in my industry?*

16.3 THE PERSONAL PROS AND CONS OF SOLO CONSULTING

Beyond the professional aspects, consulting also impacts your personal life. Weighing the personal pros and cons can help you determine whether consulting aligns with your desired lifestyle and personal values.

Personal Pros of Solo Consulting:

1. **Greater Work-Life Integration:** Consulting offers the flexibility to integrate work with your personal life, allowing you to prioritise family, hobbies, or other personal pursuits. This integration can lead to a more balanced and fulfilling lifestyle.

2. **Personal Fulfilment and Purpose:** Consulting allows you to choose work that aligns with your passions and values. The ability to make a direct impact on clients and pursue meaningful projects can lead to a greater sense of purpose and fulfilment.

3. **Opportunity for Personal Growth:** The entrepreneurial nature of consulting challenges you to develop new skills, overcome obstacles, and adapt to changing circumstances. This continuous growth can be personally rewarding and build resilience.

4. **Geographic Freedom:** Many consulting roles offer the flexibility to work remotely, providing geographic freedom. This can be ideal for those who wish to travel, relocate, or work from home without being tied to a specific location.

5. **Alignment with Personal Values:** Consulting can align closely with personal values such as independence, creativity, and the desire to help others. This alignment can lead to a more authentic and satisfying career experience.

Personal Cons of Solo Consulting:

1. **Blurred Boundaries Between Work and Personal Life:** The flexibility of consulting can sometimes lead to blurred boundaries, making it difficult to separate work from personal time. Without clear boundaries, there is a risk of overworking or experiencing burnout.

2. **Emotional Ups and Downs:** The entrepreneurial journey can be emotionally challenging, with highs and lows tied to client wins, project outcomes, and business uncertainties. Consultants must be prepared to manage the emotional aspects of self-employment.

3. **Potential for Social Isolation:** Working independently can lead to feelings of social isolation, especially if you're accustomed to a collaborative work environment. Building a supportive network and seeking out social interactions are important for maintaining well-being.

4. **Financial Stress:** The financial uncertainties of consulting can create stress, particularly if income does not meet your expectations or if unexpected expenses arise. Financial planning and having a robust financial buffer are essential for managing this stress.

5. **Time Management Challenges:** Balancing multiple roles and responsibilities can make time management challenging. Consultants must be disciplined in managing their time and prioritising tasks to avoid becoming overwhelmed.

AI Reflection Prompt: *How can I evaluate the impact of solo consulting on my personal life, including work-life balance, fulfilment, and financial security?*

16.4 A FRAMEWORK FOR DECISION-MAKING: IS SOLO CONSULTING RIGHT FOR YOU?

To make a balanced decision about whether solo consulting is right for you, use the following framework to weigh the pros and cons based on your individual circumstances:

Step 1: Define Your Priorities. Start by defining your top priorities in both your personal and professional life. What are the most important factors for you in a career—financial stability, flexibility, growth opportunities, work-life balance, or making an impact? Understanding your priorities will help you evaluate how well consulting aligns with your goals.

Step 2: List Your Pros and Cons. Create a personalised list of pros and cons for consulting based on the factors discussed in this chapter. Consider both professional and personal aspects, and be honest about your concerns and expectations.

Step 3: Assign Weight to Each Factor. Not all pros and cons carry the same weight. Assign a value or weight to each factor based on its importance to you. For example, if financial stability is a top priority, assign a higher weight to related factors. This will help you create a more nuanced evaluation.

Step 4: Evaluate the Overall Balance. Review your weighted pros and cons to evaluate the overall balance. Do the pros outweigh the cons in areas that matter most to you? Are there specific cons that you can mitigate through planning or adjustments? Use this evaluation to guide your decision-making process.

Step 5: Consider Your Readiness for Change. Reflect on your readiness for change and your willingness to embrace the uncertainties of consulting. Are you prepared to take proactive steps to address potential challenges, such as building a financial buffer, developing new skills, or seeking mentorship?

Step 6: Explore Alternatives and Contingencies. If you're uncertain about a full transition to consulting, consider alternatives such as part-time consulting (as discussed in Chapter 14) or exploring a hybrid model that combines consulting with other income streams. Having a contingency plan can provide a sense of security and flexibility as you navigate your decision.

> **AI Reflection Prompt:** *Can you guide me through a structured decision-making framework to determine whether consulting is the right path for me based on my priorities and risk tolerance?*

16.5 MAKING YOUR DECISION: NEXT STEPS

Once you've weighed the pros and cons and considered your readiness, it's time to make a decision. Whether you choose to pursue consulting, explore it part-time, or remain in your current career, the key is to make a choice that aligns with your values, goals, and unique circumstances.

- **If You Decide to Pursue Consulting:** If you choose to proceed with consulting, develop a clear plan that outlines your next steps, including financial preparation, business setup, and client acquisition strategies. Set realistic goals and milestones to guide your transition.

- **If You Decide to Wait or Explore Part-Time Options:** If you're not ready for a full transition, consider exploring consulting on a part-time basis or revisiting your decision later. Use this period to build experience, refine your skills, and gain confidence in your consulting capabilities.
- **If You Decide Consulting Isn't the Right Fit:** If consulting does not align with your current goals or circumstances, that is perfectly acceptable. Use the insights you have gained to pursue other career opportunities that better suit your needs. Remember, your career path is unique, and the best choice is one that supports your overall well-being and fulfilment.

Deciding whether to pursue solo consulting is a significant and personal decision that requires careful consideration of both the professional and personal factors involved.

By using the framework provided in this chapter, you can assess the pros and cons of consulting based on your individual circumstances and make a balanced, informed decision.

Whatever path you choose, evaluating your options is a valuable exercise in understanding your priorities, strengths, and aspirations. Consulting is not the only route to a fulfilling career, but for those who find alignment with its unique opportunities and challenges, it can be a highly rewarding journey.

> **AI Reflection Prompt:** *Based on my current level of confidence in consulting [insert current thoughts], what actionable next steps should I take to either move forward, test the waters, or revisit this decision later?*

KEY CONCEPTS

The decision to transition into consulting is highly personal and should be based on a clear evaluation of pros and cons. Consulting is not the only path to career fulfilment—choosing what aligns best with your goals and values is what matters most.

1. Understanding the Key Factors in Your Decision

Key factors influencing your decision include financial readiness, career goals, risk tolerance, work-life balance, and personal values.

A personalised evaluation framework can help determine if consulting aligns with your career and life vision.

2. Professional Pros and Cons of Solo Consulting

Pros: Autonomy, diverse project opportunities, potential for higher earnings, thought leadership, and flexible work-life balance.

Cons: Income variability, responsibility for business operations, isolation, client acquisition pressure, and lack of traditional benefits.

3. Personal Pros and Cons of Solo Consulting

Pros: Greater work-life integration, personal fulfilment, continuous growth, geographic freedom, and alignment with personal values.

Cons: Blurred work-life boundaries, emotional ups and downs, social isolation, financial stress, and time management challenges.

4. A Framework for Decision-Making: Is Solo Consulting Right for You?

Define Your Priorities: Identify key factors such as financial stability, flexibility, and professional growth.

List Your Pros and Cons: Evaluate both professional and personal aspects to gain a clear picture.

Assign Weight to Each Factor: Not all factors are equally important—prioritise what matters most.

Evaluate Overall Balance: Determine whether the benefits outweigh the challenges.

Consider Readiness for Change: Reflect on your willingness to navigate uncertainties and challenges.

Explore Alternatives: Consider part-time consulting or a hybrid approach before committing fully.

5. **Making Your Decision: Next Steps**

If you decide to pursue consulting, develop a structured plan with clear financial and business goals.

If you're uncertain, explore consulting part-time or revisit the decision later.

If consulting doesn't align with your current goals, use your insights to refine your career path.

EXERCISE: PERSONAL PROS AND CONS ANALYSIS

Step 1: Create a Pros and Cons List. Draw a two-column table with "Pros" on one side and "Cons" on the other. Based on your personal circumstances, list all the advantages (pros) and disadvantages (cons) of pursuing solo consulting.

Step 2: Prioritise Your Factors. Review your list and prioritise the pros and cons based on their impact and importance to you. Rank each factor on a scale of 1 to 5, where 1 is least important and 5 is most important.

Step 3: Reflect on Your Priorities. Consider the top three pros and the top three cons. Assess how these factors align with your values, goals, and personal situation.

Step 4: Assess Your Tolerance for the Cons. For each of the top cons, evaluate your tolerance and potential strategies to mitigate them. Are these cons manageable, or do they present significant barriers to your success in consulting?

Step 5: Make a Summary Statement. Based on your pros and cons analysis, write a summary statement about how you feel regarding consulting. Does one side clearly outweigh the other? How does this exercise impact your decision?

17: SETTING REALISTIC EXPECTATIONS

E mbarking on a consulting journey is both exciting and challenging. While the potential rewards of independence, diverse projects, and financial growth are appealing, it is essential to approach consulting with realistic expectations.

Understanding the timeline for success, anticipating potential challenges, and preparing for the ups and downs of the consulting landscape can help you navigate the path with resilience and perseverance.

In this chapter, we will discuss the importance of setting realistic expectations about consulting, including the time it takes to build a successful practice, common obstacles, and the mindset needed to thrive in this career.

17.1 THE REALITY OF CONSULTING: A MARATHON, NOT A SPRINT

The transition into consulting is often compared to running a marathon rather than a sprint. Success in consulting rarely happens overnight; it requires time, effort, and a commitment to continuous learning and adaptation. Setting realistic expectations about the timeline for achieving your goals can help you stay motivated and prevent discouragement when progress seems slow.

Key Considerations for Setting Realistic Expectations:

1. **The Initial Learning Curve:** When starting as a consultant, there is a significant learning curve that involves mastering not only your core consulting skills but also business development, client management, and operational tasks. Expect to spend time learning how to market your services, price your work, and manage client relationships effectively.

2. **Building a Client Base Takes Time:** Acquiring your first clients is often the most challenging part of starting a consulting business. It may take several months or longer to build a steady pipeline of clients, especially if you are new to consulting or shifting into a new niche. Networking, referrals, and consistent marketing efforts are essential for building momentum.

3. **Income Variability:** Financial stability in consulting typically takes time to achieve. Initial income may be unpredictable, with periods of feast and famine as you establish your client base. It is important to set realistic income expectations and have a financial buffer to support you through the early stages.

4. **Continuous Business Development:** Consulting requires ongoing business development efforts. Even after you have established a solid client base, you will need to continue marketing your services, nurturing client relationships, and seeking new opportunities. There will be times when business development feels like a full-time job in itself.

5. **Adaptation and Iteration:** The consulting market is dynamic, and success often involves adapting your services, refining your niche, and iterating on your business model. Flexibility and a willingness to pivot based on feedback and market needs are crucial for long-term success.

AI Reflection Prompt: *Based on my current skills, network, and business readiness [insert details], what would be a realistic timeline for me to establish a successful consulting practice?*

17.2 COMMON CHALLENGES IN CONSULTING

Understanding the common challenges of consulting can help you set realistic expectations and prepare strategies to overcome them. Here are some typical obstacles consultants face:

1. Client Acquisition and Retention:

Finding and retaining clients is a perennial challenge in consulting. Even seasoned consultants can experience periods of low client demand. Building strong client relationships, delivering consistent value, and maintaining an active presence in your network are key to overcoming this challenge.

Strategies for Overcoming Client Acquisition Challenges:

- Leverage Your Network: Your existing network is one of your most valuable assets. Reach out to former colleagues, industry contacts, and previous clients to generate leads and referrals.
- Demonstrate Value Early: Show potential clients the value you bring by offering initial consultations, case studies, or insights that address their specific pain points. Early demonstrations of value can build trust and increase your chances of securing new clients.
- Nurture Long-Term Relationships: Focus on building long-term relationships with your clients by staying engaged, providing exceptional service, and regularly checking in to offer ongoing support.

2. Managing Client Expectations:

Managing client expectations is critical for maintaining positive relationships and delivering successful outcomes. Misalignment between your understanding and the client's expectations can lead to dissatisfaction, scope creep, and strained relationships.

Strategies for Managing Client Expectations:

- Set Clear Expectations Upfront: Clearly outline the scope of work, deliverables, timelines, and communication protocols at the outset of the project. Use detailed proposals or contracts to document these expectations and prevent misunderstandings.
- Communicate Regularly: Regular communication is key to keeping clients informed and aligned. Provide status updates, seek feedback, and address any concerns promptly to ensure that the project stays on track.
- Be Transparent About Challenges: If unexpected challenges arise, be transparent with your client about the situation and your proposed solutions. Clients appreciate honesty and a proactive approach to problem-solving.

3. Balancing Multiple Roles:

As a solo consultant, you wear many hats, including those of service provider, marketer, salesperson, accountant, and project manager. Balancing these roles can be overwhelming and may lead to burnout if not managed effectively.

Strategies for Balancing Multiple Roles:

- Prioritise Your Tasks: Focus on high-impact tasks that drive your business forward, such as client work and business development. Use time management techniques, such as time blocking or the Eisenhower Matrix, to prioritise your activities.
- Outsource When Possible: Consider outsourcing tasks that fall outside your core expertise, such as bookkeeping, administrative work, or digital marketing. Delegating these tasks can free up your time to concentrate on client delivery and business growth.

- Set Boundaries: Establish clear boundaries between work and personal time to prevent burnout. Schedule breaks, set work hours, and use tools like project management software to keep your tasks organised and manageable.

4. Dealing with Rejection and Setbacks:

Rejection and setbacks are part of the consulting journey. Whether it's a proposal that doesn't get accepted, a client that decides not to renew, or a project that doesn't go as planned, setbacks are inevitable. Resilience and a positive mindset are essential for bouncing back and learning from these experiences.

Strategies for Dealing with Rejection and Setbacks:

- Reframe Setbacks as Learning Opportunities: View setbacks as opportunities to learn and improve. Reflect on what went wrong, what you could do differently next time, and how you can turn the experience into a valuable lesson.
- Maintain a Growth Mindset: Adopting a growth mindset—believing that skills and abilities can be developed through effort and learning—can help you stay motivated and resilient in the face of challenges.
- Celebrate Small Wins: Acknowledge and celebrate your successes, no matter how small. Recognising your achievements helps build confidence and keeps you motivated through the ups and downs.

> **AI Reflection Prompt:** *What are the biggest challenges I am likely to face in client acquisition, expectation management, and balancing multiple roles, and how can I proactively prepare for them?*

17.3 SETTING REALISTIC TIMELINES FOR SUCCESS

Success in consulting is a journey, and setting realistic timelines can help you stay focused and patient as you build your business. Here are some general timelines to consider as you set expectations for your consulting career:

Short-Term (0-6 Months):

- **Initial Learning and Setup:** Focus on setting up your consulting business, defining your niche, creating your marketing materials, and starting your networking efforts. Expect to spend this period learning about the operational aspects of consulting and laying the groundwork for client acquisition.
- **First Clients and Early Projects:** In the first few months, your goal should be to secure your first clients and complete initial projects. Use these early experiences to refine your services, build your portfolio, and gather testimonials.

Mid-Term (6-18 Months):

- **Building Momentum:** As you gain more clients and experience, your focus will shift to building momentum and establishing a steady pipeline of work. This period involves ongoing business development, refining your niche, and deepening client relationships.
- **Income Stabilisation:** By the mid-term, aim to achieve greater income stability by securing repeat clients, retainer agreements, or longer-term projects. This helps smooth out income variability and provides a more predictable revenue stream.

Long-Term (18+ Months):

- **Scaling and Growth:** In the long term, your focus will shift to scaling your consulting business. This might involve expanding your service offerings, exploring new markets, hiring subcontractors, or increasing your rates as you build a reputation and expertise.
- **Establishing Thought Leadership:** Long-term success in consulting often involves positioning yourself as a thought

leader in your field. Contribute to industry publications, speak at conferences, and create content that showcases your expertise.

AI Reflection Prompt: *Given my experience level and consulting niche [insert details], how can I set realistic short-term, mid-term, and long-term goals to measure my progress?*

17.4 CULTIVATING RESILIENCE: THRIVING THROUGH CHALLENGES

Resilience is the ability to bounce back from setbacks, adapt to change, and continue moving forward despite challenges. Cultivating resilience is essential for thriving in the consulting world, where unpredictability and obstacles are part of the journey.

Key Practices for Cultivating Resilience:

1. **Develop a Strong Support Network**: Surround yourself with supportive peers, mentors, and fellow consultants who can provide guidance, encouragement, and advice. A strong support network can help you navigate challenges and celebrate successes.
2. **Practice Self-Care:** Taking care of your physical, emotional, and mental well-being is crucial for maintaining resilience. Make time for activities that recharge you, such as exercise, meditation, hobbies, or spending time with loved ones.
3. **Embrace a Growth Mindset:** A growth mindset allows you to see challenges as opportunities for growth rather than insurmountable obstacles. Embrace learning, be open to feedback, and view each experience as a stepping stone toward your goals.
4. **Set Realistic Goals and Milestones:** Setting achievable goals and celebrating small milestones can help you maintain momentum and stay motivated. Break down larger goals into manageable steps and track your progress regularly.
5. **Stay Flexible and Open to Change:** The ability to pivot and adapt is a key component of resilience. Stay open to new

opportunities, be willing to adjust your approach, and view change as a natural part of the consulting journey.

AI Reflection Prompt: *What strategies can I implement to build resilience and maintain motivation through the inevitable ups and downs of consulting?*

Setting realistic expectations regarding the timeline for success, potential challenges, and the need for resilience is essential for a fulfilling and sustainable consulting career. By approaching consulting with a clear understanding of the journey ahead, you can navigate the ups and downs with confidence, perseverance, and a growth-oriented mindset.

Success in consulting is not defined by a single metric but by the cumulative progress you make over time. By setting realistic expectations, preparing for challenges, and cultivating resilience, you can create a consulting practice that aligns with your goals, values, and vision for your professional life.

KEY CONCEPTS

Consulting success requires realistic expectations, persistence, and resilience. The journey has its ups and downs, but a clear strategy and adaptability enhance long-term success. Setting realistic goals, preparing for challenges, and maintaining a strong mindset are essential for a fulfilling and sustainable consulting career.

1. **Consulting is a Marathon, Not a Sprint**

Success takes time, requiring patience, persistence, and continuous learning.

Expect an initial learning curve in business operations, marketing, and client management.

Building a client base and achieving income stability can take several months or longer.

Business development is an ongoing process—consultants must consistently market their services.

Flexibility and adaptation are key to long-term sustainability in consulting.

2. Common Challenges in Consulting

Client Acquisition and Retention: Finding and keeping clients requires networking, demonstrating value early, and nurturing relationships.

Managing Client Expectations: Clear communication, setting boundaries, and aligning expectations upfront prevent misunderstandings and scope creep.

Balancing Multiple Roles: Consultants must juggle client work, marketing, financial management, and operations. Prioritisation, outsourcing, and boundary-setting are crucial.

Handling Rejection and Setbacks: Resilience is needed to manage client losses, unsuccessful proposals, and fluctuating work demand.

3. Setting Realistic Timelines for Success

0-6 months: Initial learning, setup, networking, and securing first clients.

6-18 months: Establishing momentum, refining services, and stabilising income.

18+ months: Scaling, increasing rates, exploring new opportunities, and building a strong industry presence.

4. Cultivating Resilience to Thrive in Consulting

Build a strong support network of peers, mentors, and other consultants.

Prioritise self-care and work-life balance to avoid burnout.

Embrace a growth mindset—learn from setbacks and continuously improve.

Set achievable goals and celebrate small wins to maintain motivation.

Stay flexible and adaptable in response to market changes and opportunities.

EXERCISE: REALITY CHECK ON EXPECTATIONS

Step 1: List Your Expectations. Write down your current expectations about consulting, including potential income, work-life balance, client relationships, and the overall consulting experience.

Step 2: Assess the Realism of Each Expectation. For each expectation, rate its realism on a scale of 1 to 5, where 1 means not realistic at all and 5 means very realistic. Consider how each expectation aligns with what you have learned about consulting so far.

Step 3: Identify Potential Gaps. Identify any gaps between your expectations and the realities of consulting. For expectations rated lower in realism, consider why they might be unrealistic and what adjustments could be made.

Step 4: Adjust Your Expectations. Rewrite each expectation to make it more realistic, based on your new insights. For example, if you originally expected a steady income immediately, adjust this to reflect the potential for variability, especially in the early stages.

Step 5: Reflect on Adjustments. Reflect on how adjusting your expectations impacts your view of consulting. How does setting more realistic expectations help you feel more prepared and confident about this path?

18: LISTENING TO YOUR INTUITION AND PROFESSIONAL GOALS

Deciding whether to pursue solo consulting is not merely a matter of weighing pros and cons or analysing market opportunities; it also involves aligning your decision with your deeper professional and personal goals.

Beyond rational analysis, your intuition and inner sense of purpose play a crucial role in guiding your career choices.

In this chapter, we will explore the importance of listening to your intuition, aligning your decision with your broader goals, and trusting your instincts when evaluating whether consulting is the right path for you.

18.1 THE ROLE OF INTUITION IN DECISION-MAKING

Intuition is often described as the ability to understand something immediately, without the need for conscious reasoning. It is a powerful tool that taps into your accumulated knowledge, experiences, and inner wisdom.

While intuition alone should not be the sole basis for major decisions, it serves as a valuable complement to rational analysis.

Why Intuition Matters:

- **Guidance Beyond Data:** Intuition provides guidance in areas where data may be limited or when decisions involve personal values and emotions that are difficult to quantify.
- **Tapping Into Experience:** Your intuition is shaped by your past experiences, successes, challenges, and observations. It reflects a deeper understanding of what feels right or wrong based on your unique journey.
- **Connecting with Your Values:** Intuition helps you connect with your core values and motivations, ensuring that your decisions are aligned with what truly matters to you.

AI Reflection Prompt: *How can I recognise and interpret my intuition when considering whether solo consulting is the right career move for me?*

18.2 ALIGNING YOUR DECISION WITH PROFESSIONAL AND PERSONAL GOALS

To make a decision that feels right for you, it is important to align your choice with your broader professional and personal goals. Consulting may offer many benefits, but it is crucial to assess whether it supports your vision for your life and career.

Steps to Align Your Decision:

1. Reflect on Your Professional Goals

Take time to reflect on your professional goals and how consulting fits into that picture. Consider both your short-term and long-term aspirations, such as:

- **Career Growth:** Does consulting offer the growth opportunities you seek? Are there skills you want to develop, experiences you want to gain, or achievements you want to pursue that consulting can provide?
- **Impact and Contribution**: Reflect on the impact you want to make through your work. Does consulting allow you to

contribute in a meaningful way, whether it's solving complex problems, helping others, or driving innovation in your field?

Recognition and Expertise: Consider whether consulting aligns with your desire for recognition or to be seen as an expert in your field. Consulting can offer platforms for thought leadership, but it requires proactive effort to build your brand and reputation.

2. Consider Your Personal Goals and Values

Your career choices are deeply intertwined with your personal life and values. Ensure that consulting aligns with your overall vision for how you want to live and what you value most.

- **Work-Life Balance:** Evaluate whether consulting supports the work-life balance you desire. Are you looking for more time with family, flexibility in your schedule, or the ability to pursue personal interests? Consulting's flexibility can be an asset, but it requires discipline to maintain boundaries.
- **Financial Security:** Consider your financial goals and how consulting fits into your plans for financial stability and growth. Are you comfortable with the financial uncertainties of consulting, and do you have a strategy to manage them?
- **Fulfilment and Happiness:** Reflect on what brings you fulfilment and happiness in your work. Does consulting align with your passions and provide a sense of purpose? Your career should be a source of joy and motivation, not just a means to an end.

3. Identify Non-Negotiables

Identify your non-negotiables—the aspects of your career and life that you are not willing to compromise. Non-negotiables can include things like time with loved ones, health and well-being, or the ability to work on projects that align with your values. Use these non-negotiables as a guide to ensure that your decision aligns with your core needs.

4. Visualise Your Future as a Consultant

Visualisation is a powerful tool for aligning your decision with your goals and intuition. Spend time visualising what your life would look like as a consultant. Imagine your daily routines, the types of projects you'd work on, the clients you'd serve, and how you'd feel in this role.

- **Envision Success:** Picture yourself succeeding as a consultant. How does it feel? What does success look like for you, and how does it align with your professional and personal aspirations?
- **Anticipate Challenges:** Visualise potential challenges as well. Consider how you would handle obstacles, such as client acquisition or income variability. Does the prospect of overcoming these challenges excite you, or does it feel burdensome?

   AI Reflection Prompt: *Based on my career and personal goals [insert your goals], how well does consulting align with my vision for professional growth, impact, financial stability, and work-life balance?*

18.3 TRUSTING YOUR INSTINCTS: LISTENING TO THE INNER VOICE

While analysis and planning are critical components of decision-making, it is equally important to trust your instincts. Your inner voice often knows what is right for you, even when the path is not entirely clear.

How to Tune into Your Intuition:

1. **Create Space for Reflection:** Give yourself time and space to reflect on your decision without external distractions. Quiet moments, meditation, or journaling can help you connect with your intuition and gain clarity.
2. **Notice How You Feel:** Pay attention to your emotions and physical responses when you think about consulting. Does the idea energise you, or do you feel anxious and hesitant? Your

emotional reactions can provide valuable insights into your true feelings about consulting.

3. **Listen to Repeated Signals:** Intuition often communicates through repeated signals or gut feelings. If you find yourself consistently drawn to the idea of consulting or feeling a sense of excitement about the possibilities, take note of these signals.

4. **Seek Inner Alignment:** Consider whether your decision feels aligned with your authentic self. Are you making this choice because it aligns with your true desires, or are you influenced by external pressures, such as societal expectations or the opinions of others?

AI Reflection Prompt: *When I reflect on consulting as a career path, what recurring thoughts, emotions, or physical reactions do I experience, and what might they be signalling about my readiness for this transition?*

18.4 BALANCING INTUITION WITH RATIONAL DECISION-MAKING

While intuition is a valuable guide, it is important to balance it with rational decision-making. Use intuition to inform your choices, but also ensure that your decision is grounded in practical considerations and thorough analysis.

Balancing Intuition and Rationality:

- **Validate Your Intuition with Data:** If your intuition points you toward consulting, validate it with data and research. Assess market demand, financial feasibility, and alignment with your skills to ensure that your decision is both inspired and practical.
- **Use a Decision Matrix:** A decision matrix can help you weigh the pros and cons of consulting in a structured way. Include both rational factors, such as income potential and market demand, and intuitive factors, such as alignment with values and personal fulfilment.
- **Seek Input from Trusted Advisors:** While your decision is ultimately yours, seeking input from trusted advisors, mentors,

or colleagues can provide additional perspectives. Be mindful to choose advisors who understand your goals and respect your intuition.

AI Reflection Prompt: *How can I combine intuition with logical analysis to ensure that my decision about consulting is both personally fulfilling and financially viable?*

18.5 MAKING PEACE WITH YOUR DECISION

Once you've evaluated your options, listened to your intuition, and aligned your decision with your goals, it's time to make peace with your choice. Whether you decide to pursue consulting, explore it part-time, or choose a different path, trust that you've made the best decision for your unique circumstances.

Steps to Make Peace with Your Decision:

1. **Own Your Choice:** Take ownership of your decision, recognising that it's based on a thoughtful evaluation of your goals, values, and intuition. Embrace your choice with confidence and commit to making it work for you.
2. **Let Go of Doubts:** It's natural to have doubts, especially when making significant career changes. Acknowledge your doubts, but don't let them undermine your confidence. Trust that you have the ability to adapt and succeed in whatever path you choose.
3. **Stay Open to Reassessment:** Your decision is not set in stone. Stay open to reassessing your path as you gain new experiences and insights. Flexibility allows you to make adjustments and pivot as needed, ensuring that your career remains aligned with your evolving goals.
4. **Celebrate Your Courage:** Making a career decision that aligns with your true self requires courage. Celebrate your willingness to explore new possibilities and trust your instincts. Whether consulting is the right path now or in the

future, your commitment to living authentically is a success in itself.

AI Reflection Prompt: *What steps can I take to fully commit to my decision —whether to pursue, delay, or reconsider consulting—while remaining open to reassessment in the future?*

Listening to your intuition and aligning your decision with your deeper professional and personal goals is a powerful approach to making career choices. Consulting is not just a professional decision— it's a personal journey that should resonate with your values, aspirations, and sense of purpose.

By tuning into your intuition, reflecting on your goals, and trusting your instincts, you can make a decision that feels right for you. Whether you choose to pursue consulting or another path, the key is to honour your inner voice and create a career that supports your vision for your life. Trust yourself, stay true to your goals, and embrace the journey with confidence and optimism.

KEY CONCEPTS

Consulting is not just a professional decision—it's a personal journey that should align with your values, aspirations, and intuition. Trusting yourself and making choices that support your vision for life is essential for long-term fulfilment.

1. The Role of Intuition in Decision-Making

Intuition is a valuable tool that draws from your experiences, emotions, and subconscious knowledge.

It complements rational analysis by guiding decisions where data is limited or personal values are involved.

Tuning into intuition helps ensure career choices align with your deeper motivations.

2. Aligning Your Decision with Professional and Personal Goals

Reflect on the career growth, impact, and thought leadership opportunities that consulting may provide.

Consider personal priorities such as work-life balance, financial stability, and fulfilment.

Identify non-negotiables—what aspects of work and life you are unwilling to compromise.

Visualise your life as a consultant, considering both the opportunities and challenges.

3. Trusting Your Instincts: Listening to the Inner Voice

Create space for self-reflection through quiet moments, journaling, or meditation.

Pay attention to your emotional and physical reactions when contemplating consulting.

Look for repeated signals—persistent excitement or doubt can be indicators.

Ensure your decision aligns with your authentic self, rather than external pressures.

4. Balancing Intuition with Rational Decision-Making

Validate your intuition with data by researching market demand, financial feasibility, and skill alignment.

Use a decision matrix to weigh logical and intuitive factors side by side.

Seek input from trusted advisors, while ensuring the final decision reflects your personal goals.

5. Making Peace with Your Decision

Fully commit to your choice and own it with confidence.

Let go of self-doubt while remaining open to reassessment as new insights emerge.

Celebrate your courage in making a career decision based on both intuition and thoughtful evaluation.

EXERCISE: INTUITION AND GOAL ALIGNMENT EXERCISE

Step 1: Revisit Your Professional Goals. List your top professional and personal goals. Be specific about what you hope to achieve in your career and how you want your work to align with your life values.

Step 2: Reflect on Intuition. Take a quiet moment to reflect on your intuition regarding consulting. Consider how you feel about consulting at a gut level, beyond logical analysis. Write down any intuitive thoughts, feelings, or reactions that arise.

Step 3: Match Consulting to Your Goals. Compare your professional goals with the consulting path. Identify areas of alignment and misalignment. Consider how consulting can help you achieve your goals or where it might fall short.

Step 4: Write an Intuitive Reflection. Write a brief intuitive reflection on your decision. Use phrases like "My gut tells me…" or "I feel most aligned when…" to capture your intuitive response.

Step 5: Create an Actionable Insight. Based on your reflection, write one actionable insight or step that honours both your professional goals and intuition. This might include further exploration, a small trial run in consulting, or a decision to pause and reassess.

19: SEEKING ADVICE AND MENTORSHIP

Transitioning into solo consulting can feel overwhelming, especially when faced with the numerous decisions and uncertainties involved in starting your own practice.

One of the most valuable resources available during this journey is the advice and mentorship of those who have already walked the path you're considering. Connecting with experienced consultants or mentors in your field can provide clarity, practical insights, and guidance that extends beyond theoretical knowledge.

In this chapter, we'll explore the importance of seeking advice and mentorship and provide strategies for finding and building meaningful relationships with mentors who can support your consulting journey.

19.1 THE VALUE OF ADVICE AND MENTORSHIP IN CONSULTING

Mentorship offers a wealth of benefits, particularly for those entering the consulting field. A mentor can provide guidance on navigating the complexities of consulting, share valuable lessons from their own experiences, and help you avoid common pitfalls. Beyond practical advice, mentors also offer emotional support, encouragement, and a sense of connection in what can sometimes be an isolating career.

Key Benefits of Seeking Advice and Mentorship:

1. **Gaining Real-World Insights:** Mentors provide practical, real-world insights that go beyond what you can learn from books, courses, or online resources. They can offer context, share their personal experiences, and provide actionable advice tailored to your specific situation.
2. **Expanding Your Network:** A mentor can introduce you to their network, helping you connect with potential clients, collaborators, or other consultants who can further support your business. Networking through mentorship opens doors that might otherwise be difficult to access on your own.
3. **Accelerating Your Learning Curve:** Having a mentor can significantly shorten your learning curve by guiding you through the early stages of consulting. They can help you navigate challenges, identify opportunities, and refine your strategies more quickly than if you were figuring everything out alone.
4. **Providing Accountability and Encouragement:** A mentor can serve as an accountability partner, helping you stay focused on your goals and offering encouragement when you encounter setbacks. Their support can boost your confidence and keep you motivated through the ups and downs of consulting.
5. **Offering a Different Perspective:** Mentors can provide an outside perspective that challenges your assumptions and broadens your thinking. They can help you see blind spots, consider alternative approaches, and make more informed decisions.

AI Reflection Prompt: *How can I identify the key areas where mentorship would benefit me the most in my consulting journey, and what qualities should I look for in a mentor?*

19.2 STRATEGIES FOR FINDING THE RIGHT MENTOR

Finding the right mentor involves identifying individuals who possess the experience, knowledge, and willingness to guide you. Here are strategies to help you find a mentor who aligns with your needs and goals:

1. Leverage Your Existing Network

Start by exploring your existing network for potential mentors. This could include former colleagues, managers, professors, or industry contacts who have experience in consulting or who have navigated similar career transitions.

- **Reach Out with a Clear Request:** When approaching potential mentors within your network, be specific about what you seek. Whether it's guidance on starting a consulting business, advice on a particular niche, or general career insights, a clear request makes it easier for them to understand how they can help.
- **Start Informally:** If you're unsure about a formal mentorship, begin with an informal conversation or a coffee meeting. This approach allows both parties to get to know each other and assess whether there's a good fit before committing to a more structured mentorship.

2. Join Professional Organisations and Associations

Professional organisations and industry associations often have mentorship programs or networking events that facilitate connections between experienced professionals and those new to the field.

- **Participate Actively:** Engage actively in professional organisations by attending events, joining committees, or volunteering. Active participation increases your visibility and provides opportunities to meet potential mentors who share your interests.
- **Look for Mentorship Programs:** Many organisations offer formal mentorship programs designed to connect experienced

professionals with newcomers. These programs can be an excellent way to find mentors who are committed to supporting the next generation of consultants.

3. Use Online Platforms and Communities

Online platforms such as LinkedIn, industry-specific forums, or social media groups can be valuable resources for finding mentors. These platforms enable you to connect with consultants and experts from around the world.

- **Engage with Content and Discussions:** Follow consultants and thought leaders in your field, engage with their content, and participate in discussions. This can help you build relationships organically and identify individuals who resonate with your goals.
- **Reach Out Directly:** Don't hesitate to contact consultants whose work you admire, even if you don't have a prior connection. A respectful and thoughtful message expressing your appreciation for their work and a specific request for guidance can open the door to mentorship.

4. Attend Conferences, Workshops, and Webinars

Conferences, workshops, and webinars are excellent opportunities to meet potential mentors and learn from industry experts. These events provide a platform for networking, sharing ideas, and building relationships.

- **Network Proactively:** Approach speakers, panellists, or attendees who have experience in consulting. Express your interest in their insights and ask if they would be open to staying in touch or offering advice.
- **Participate in Q&A Sessions:** Use Q&A sessions at events to ask thoughtful questions and engage with experts. This not only provides valuable insights but also helps you stand out and connect with those who share your interests.

5. Explore Mentorship Platforms

There are several platforms dedicated to connecting mentees with mentors across various industries. Websites like MentorCity, SCORE, and Ten Thousand Coffees offer mentorship matching services that can help you find a mentor with the right expertise.

- **Create a Detailed Profile:** When using mentorship platforms, create a detailed profile that outlines your background, goals, and what you are seeking in a mentor. A well-crafted profile increases your chances of being matched with a mentor who aligns with your needs.
- **Be Open to Virtual Mentorship:** Many mentorship platforms offer virtual mentoring, allowing you to connect with mentors regardless of geographic location. Virtual mentorship can be just as impactful as in-person guidance, providing flexibility and access to a broader pool of mentors.

AI Reflection Prompt: *Based on my consulting niche and goals [insert niche/goals], what are the best ways for me to find and connect with potential mentors who can provide relevant guidance?*

19.3 BUILDING A STRONG MENTORSHIP RELATIONSHIP

Once you have identified a potential mentor, the next step is to build a strong, mutually beneficial relationship. Successful mentorship relationships are built on trust, respect, and open communication.

Tips for Building a Strong Mentorship Relationship:

1. **Set Clear Expectations:** At the outset, discuss and agree on the expectations for your mentorship relationship. This includes the frequency and format of meetings, the topics you want to cover, and any specific goals you hope to achieve through mentorship.
2. **Be Proactive and Prepared:** Take the initiative in scheduling meetings, setting agendas, and following up on action items.

Come to each meeting prepared with questions, discussion topics, and updates on your progress. Proactivity shows your mentor that you value their time and are committed to the mentorship.

3. **Be Open to Feedback:** One of the key benefits of mentorship is receiving constructive feedback. Be open to your mentor's suggestions, even if they challenge your current thinking. Use feedback as an opportunity to learn, grow, and refine your approach.

4. **Show Appreciation:** Express your gratitude for your mentor's time, insights, and support. A simple thank-you note, an acknowledgment of their impact on your progress, or a small gesture of appreciation can go a long way in strengthening your relationship.

5. **Maintain Regular Communication:** Regular communication is crucial for keeping the mentorship relationship active and productive. Whether through scheduled meetings, email updates, or quick check-ins, staying in touch helps maintain momentum and ensures ongoing support.

6. **Be Respectful of Boundaries:** While mentors are there to guide and support you, it's important to respect their boundaries and time. Avoid overwhelming them with excessive requests or expecting them to have all the answers. A balanced and respectful approach fosters a positive and sustainable mentorship.

AI Reflection Prompt: *How can I structure and maintain a productive mentorship relationship, ensuring that I maximise learning while respecting my mentor's time?*

19.4 GIVING BACK: THE RECIPROCAL NATURE OF MENTORSHIP

While mentorship often focuses on the benefits to the mentee, it's important to recognise that mentorship is a reciprocal relationship. Mentors also gain from the experience through personal satisfaction, the opportunity to give back, and the chance to learn from fresh perspectives.

Ways to Give Back to Your Mentor:

1. **Share Your Progress:** Keep your mentor updated on your achievements, milestones, and how their advice has helped you. Sharing your success not only validates their investment in you but also provides them with a sense of fulfilment.
2. **Offer Your Support:** Be open to offering your support in areas where you can add value. This could include providing insights from your own experiences, assisting with projects, or connecting them with your network when relevant.
3. **Acknowledge Their Impact Publicly:** Publicly acknowledging your mentor's impact, whether through social media, a professional platform, or a recommendation, is a meaningful way to show appreciation and highlight their contributions.
4. **Consider Becoming a Mentor Yourself:** As you gain experience and grow in your consulting career, consider paying it forward by mentoring others. Sharing your journey and insights with new consultants or professionals entering the field continues the cycle of support and growth.

AI Reflection Prompt: What steps can I take to provide value to my mentor and contribute to the mentorship relationship in a meaningful way?

19.5 NAVIGATING CHALLENGES IN MENTORSHIP

While mentorship can be highly beneficial, it's not without its challenges. It's important to approach mentorship with flexibility and a willingness to navigate any issues that arise.

Common Challenges and How to Address Them:

1. **Misalignment of Expectations:** If you and your mentor have different expectations, it can lead to misunderstandings or frustration. Address this by having an open conversation about

your needs, adjusting your approach, or seeking a mentor better suited to your goals.

2. **Scheduling Conflicts:** Busy schedules can make it difficult to maintain regular communication. Be flexible and proactive in finding meeting times that work for both parties, and consider alternative formats, such as email check-ins or phone calls, if needed.

3. **Evolving Needs:** As you progress in your consulting journey, your needs may change, and you may require different types of guidance. It's okay to seek additional mentors or to transition out of a mentorship if it no longer aligns with your goals.

Seeking advice and mentorship is a powerful way to gain clarity, practical insights, and support as you explore the path of solo consulting. By connecting with experienced consultants or mentors, you can accelerate your learning, expand your network, and navigate the challenges of consulting with confidence.

Mentorship is a two-way street, built on trust, respect, and mutual benefit. Approach mentorship with an open mind, a proactive attitude, and a commitment to growth. Whether you're receiving guidance or giving back, mentorship enriches both your professional journey and the broader consulting community.

> **AI Reflection Prompt:** *If I encounter challenges such as mismatched expectations or scheduling difficulties with a mentor, what are the best ways to address and navigate these issues effectively?*

KEY CONCEPTS

Seeking mentorship accelerates your learning and provides critical support as you navigate consulting. A strong mentorship relationship is built on mutual respect, clear communication, and shared learning. Giving back to the mentorship ecosystem ensures continuous growth for both mentors and mentees.

1. The Value of Advice and Mentorship in Consulting

Mentorship provides real-world insights, shortens the learning curve, and helps navigate challenges.

A mentor can expand your network and introduce you to new opportunities.

Having a mentor offers accountability, encouragement, and an outside perspective to refine your approach.

2. Strategies for Finding the Right Mentor

Leverage Your Existing Network: Reach out to former colleagues, managers, or industry contacts.

Join Professional Organisations: Participate in industry associations and mentorship programs.

Use Online Platforms: Engage with consultants on LinkedIn and industry-specific forums.

Attend Conferences & Events: Network at industry gatherings to connect with experienced professionals.

3. Building a Strong Mentorship Relationship

Set clear expectations regarding goals, meeting frequency, and areas of guidance.

Be proactive—schedule meetings, come prepared with questions, and follow up on action items.

Accept constructive feedback and use it to refine your approach.

Show appreciation for your mentor's time and insights.

Maintain regular communication while respecting their time and boundaries.

4. Giving Back: The Reciprocal Nature of Mentorship

Keep your mentor updated on how their advice has helped you.

Offer your support where possible—introducing contacts, sharing insights, or assisting with projects.

Publicly acknowledge your mentor's impact through social media or recommendations.

Consider becoming a mentor yourself as you gain experience, thus continuing the cycle of support.

5. Navigating Challenges in Mentorship

Mismatched Expectations: Engage in open conversations to clarify goals and ensure alignment.

Scheduling Conflicts: Be flexible and find ways to stay in touch through emails or shorter meetings.

Evolving Needs: Seek additional mentors as your consulting journey progresses.

EXERCISE: BUILDING YOUR SUPPORT NETWORK

Step 1: Identify Potential Mentors and Advisors. List people in your network who have experience in consulting or can offer valuable guidance. Include former colleagues, industry contacts, or even individuals you admire from a distance.

Step 2: Plan Your Outreach. For each person on your list, plan how you will approach them for advice or mentorship. Consider what specific questions or topics you would like to discuss, such as their consulting journey, challenges they faced, or advice they would offer to someone starting out.

Step 3: Draft Outreach Messages. Write draft messages or conversation starters for reaching out to these individuals. Be clear about your intent, show appreciation for their expertise, and specify what you are seeking (e.g., a brief coffee chat, a phone call, or insights via email).

Step 4: Schedule and Engage. Set a timeline for reaching out to each person and schedule your conversations. After each interaction, take notes on key insights, advice, and any reflections that impact your decision-making process.

Step 5: Reflect on Your Conversations. Reflect on the advice and perspectives you gathered from your support network. How do these insights align with your own thoughts and feelings about consulting? Did any advice surprise you or shift your thinking?

20: MAKING THE FINAL DECISION: A PERSONAL REFLECTION

After exploring the many facets of solo consulting—including its rewards, challenges, market opportunities, and alignment with your personal and professional goals—you are now at the crucial point of making your final decision.

Whether you're leaning towards pursuing consulting, exploring it part-time, or opting for a different path, it's essential to consolidate your thoughts and weigh all factors carefully.

This chapter provides a guided reflection exercise designed to help you bring together everything you've learned, listen to your inner voice, and make a confident decision about whether to pursue solo consulting.

20.1 THE IMPORTANCE OF A REFLECTIVE DECISION-MAKING PROCESS

Reflective decision-making involves pausing, stepping back, and thoughtfully considering all aspects of a choice. This process goes beyond simply weighing pros and cons; it includes connecting with your deeper motivations, values, and intuition. By engaging in a reflective exercise, you can gain clarity, reduce uncertainty, and make a decision that feels right for you on both a personal and professional level.

Benefits of Reflective Decision-Making:

- **Clarity:** Reflection helps you clarify your thoughts, prioritise what matters most, and view your options from a balanced perspective.
- **Confidence:** By thoroughly evaluating your decision, you build confidence in your choice, reducing doubts and second-guessing.
- **Alignment:** Reflecting on your decision ensures that it aligns with your overall vision for your life and career, leading to greater fulfilment and satisfaction.

AI Reflection Prompt: *How can I structure my decision-making process to ensure that my choice about consulting aligns with both logic and my deeper personal and professional values?*

20.2 A GUIDED REFLECTION EXERCISE: DECIDING ON SOLO CONSULTING

This guided reflection exercise is designed to help you consolidate your thoughts and feelings about pursuing solo consulting. Set aside some quiet time and space to work through these steps thoughtfully, allowing yourself to explore your true feelings and insights.

Step 1: Revisit Your Why. Begin by revisiting the core reasons you are considering solo consulting. Reflect on the motivations that have drawn you to this path.

Questions to Consider:

- Why am I considering solo consulting?
- What excites me most about the prospect of consulting?
- How does consulting align with my core values and professional aspirations?

Write down your answers, focusing on the emotions and motivations that resonate most deeply with you. Understanding your "why" provides a foundation for your decision and helps keep you anchored to your true intentions.

Step 2: Weigh the Pros and Cons. Next, take a moment to weigh the pros and cons of consulting, incorporating both practical considerations and your personal reflections.

Action:

- Create a list of the pros and cons of solo consulting as they relate to your specific situation.
- Rank each item by its importance to you. For example, a con like "income variability" may be a minor concern if you have a robust financial buffer, whereas "flexibility" may rank highly if work-life balance is a top priority.

Reflect on your ranked list. Are the pros compelling enough to outweigh the cons? Are the cons manageable with the right strategies and support? Use this analysis to assess whether the benefits of consulting align with your most important priorities.

Step 3: Assess Your Readiness. Evaluate your readiness for consulting by considering both your practical preparedness and emotional readiness. Consulting requires not only skills and resources but also the right mindset and resilience.

Questions to Consider:

- Am I financially prepared for potential variability in consulting income?
- Do I have the skills, support, and resources needed to start my consulting business?
- How do I feel about the challenges of consulting, such as client acquisition, self-management, and wearing multiple hats?

Rate your readiness on a scale from 1 to 10, with 10 being fully prepared and confident. If your rating is lower than you would like, consider what steps you can take to increase your readiness. This might include further skill development, financial planning, or seeking mentorship.

Step 4: Envision Your Consulting Life. Visualisation is a powerful tool for connecting with your intuition and assessing how a decision aligns with your goals. Envision your life as a solo consultant and explore how it feels.

Visualisation Exercise:

- Close your eyes and imagine a typical day as a solo consultant. Picture your work environment, the types of clients you work with, and the projects you engage in.
- Consider how you feel during this day. Are you energised, fulfilled, and motivated? Or do you feel stressed, overwhelmed, or uncertain?

Take note of your emotional responses during this visualisation. Your feelings can provide valuable insights into whether consulting resonates with your ideal vision for your career and lifestyle.

Step 5: Reflect on Your Intuition. Your intuition is a powerful guide that reflects your inner wisdom and accumulated experiences. Take a moment to tune into your gut feelings about consulting.

Questions to Consider:

- What does my intuition tell me about consulting? Do I feel a sense of excitement, peace, or alignment?
- Are there any lingering doubts or concerns that my intuition is highlighting?

Trust your gut feelings, even if they do not fully align with logical analysis. Your intuition often knows what is best for you on a deeper level, guiding you towards choices that feel authentic and fulfilling.

Step 6: Explore Alternatives and Contingency Plans. Consider alternatives or contingency plans that can provide flexibility and reduce the pressure of an all-or-nothing decision. Exploring part-time consulting, starting with small projects, or maintaining a hybrid model can be effective ways to ease into consulting.

Questions to Consider:

- What alternatives can I explore if I'm not ready to fully commit to consulting?
- How can I test the waters or create a gradual transition into consulting?

Having a contingency plan can offer reassurance and flexibility, allowing you to pursue consulting at a pace that feels comfortable and manageable.

Step 7: Make Your Decision. After reflecting on the above steps, it's time to make your decision. Whether you choose to pursue consulting, explore it gradually, or determine that it's not the right path for you, embrace your decision with confidence and commitment.

Final Reflection:

- Based on everything I've reflected on, what feels like the right decision for me?
- How can I move forward with confidence, knowing that I've thoughtfully considered all factors?

Write down your decision and the reasons behind it. Committing your choice to writing can solidify your decision and serve as a reminder of the thoughtful process you undertook to reach it.

> **AI Reflection Prompt:** *Can you guide me through a structured reflection exercise to help me assess whether solo consulting is the right path for me, considering my motivations, pros and cons, readiness, and intuition?*

20.3 MOVING FORWARD WITH CONFIDENCE

Once you've made your decision, it's important to move forward with confidence, regardless of the path you've chosen. Trust that you have made the best choice for your unique circumstances and that your journey is guided by your values, goals, and intuition.

Tips for Moving Forward:

- **Commit Fully to Your Decision:** Whether you're diving into consulting, exploring it part-time, or choosing a different path, commit fully to your decision. A focused and committed approach will maximise your chances of success and satisfaction.
- **Embrace Flexibility:** Remember that your career journey is not linear, and it's okay to adjust your path as needed. Stay open to new opportunities, remain flexible, and be willing to pivot if your goals or circumstances change.
- **Celebrate Your Decision:** Celebrate the clarity and confidence you've gained through this reflective process. Acknowledge the courage it takes to make a career decision that aligns with your true self, and take pride in your commitment to living authentically.

Deciding whether to pursue solo consulting is a deeply personal and significant choice. By engaging in guided reflection, you can consolidate your thoughts, connect with your intuition, and make a decision that aligns with your professional and personal goals. Whether you choose consulting, explore it part-time, or decide on a different path, trust that your journey is uniquely yours and that your decision reflects your authentic self.

Your career is a reflection of your values, aspirations, and strengths. Embrace your decision with confidence, knowing that you are equipped to navigate whatever path you choose with resilience, purpose, and clarity. Your journey is just beginning, and the choices you make today set the foundation for a fulfilling and rewarding future.

> **AI Reflection Prompt:** *Now that I have made a decision about consulting, how can I fully commit to it while remaining flexible and confident in my choice?*

KEY CONCEPTS

Making a decision about consulting requires a balance of logic, intuition, and personal reflection. Whatever choice you make, trust that it aligns with your goals and circumstances at this moment.

1. The Importance of a Reflective Decision-Making Process

Decision-making should involve deep reflection beyond just the pros and cons.

Reflection brings clarity, builds confidence, and ensures alignment with personal and professional goals.

2. A Guided Reflection Exercise: Deciding on Solo Consulting

Revisit Your Why: Identify what excites you about consulting and how it aligns with your values.

Weigh the Pros and Cons: List and rank the advantages and challenges of consulting based on their importance.

Assess Your Readiness: Evaluate your financial, emotional, and skill-based preparedness.

Visualise Your Consulting Life: Imagine a typical consulting day and assess your emotional response.

Listen to Your Intuition: Identify any gut feelings or recurring doubts.

Explore Alternatives: Consider part-time consulting or phased transitions as alternatives.

Make Your Decision: Write down and commit to your choice, clarifying your reasons.

3. **Moving Forward with Confidence**

Fully commit to your decision, whether it is consulting, a hybrid approach, or staying in your current career.

Embrace flexibility, knowing you can adjust your path over time.

Celebrate the decision-making process as a step towards a fulfilling career.

EXERCISE: GUIDED DECISION-MAKING REFLECTION

Step 1: Summarise Your Journey So Far. Write a summary of your journey through the decision-making process. Highlight key insights, moments of clarity, or significant challenges you have faced. Consider both the logical and emotional aspects of your decision.

Step 2: Evaluate Your Readiness to Decide. Assess how ready you feel to make a final decision on a scale of 1 to 10, where 1 means not ready at all and 10 means completely ready. Reflect on what you need to move closer to a confident decision.

Step 3: Address Remaining Questions. List any remaining questions or uncertainties that are holding you back from making a decision. For each question, identify steps you can take to seek answers or reduce uncertainty, such as further research, additional conversations, or self-reflection.

Step 4: Visualise Both Paths. Spend a few minutes visualising each path—one where you pursue consulting and one where you continue on your current trajectory. Reflect on how each path feels, what excites or concerns you, and which aligns more closely with your values and goals.

Step 5: Make a Decision Statement. Based on your reflections, write a decision statement. This could be a commitment to pursue consulting, a plan to explore further, or a decision to stay in your current role. Include the reasons for your choice and how it aligns with your overall vision.

Step 6: Plan Your Next Steps. Outline the immediate next steps based on your decision statement. This may include actions to start your consulting journey, further exploration activities, or steps to enhance your current role.

PART 5: PREPARING FOR THE TRANSITION

(WITHOUT GOING TOO DEEP)

The secret of getting ahead is getting started.

MARK TWAIN

21: CREATING A PRELIMINARY TRANSITION PLAN

Deciding to transition into solo consulting is a significant step, and having a preliminary plan can help you navigate this change with greater confidence and clarity.

While your detailed business plan will come later, starting with a basic transition plan can set you on the right path by focusing on key areas such as mindset shifts, initial financial planning, and setting personal milestones.

This chapter outlines the foundational steps you need to consider as you begin preparing for your transition into consulting.

21.1 SHIFTING YOUR MINDSET: FROM EMPLOYEE TO ENTREPRENEUR

Transitioning from a traditional employment role to solo consulting necessitates more than just logistical preparation; it requires a shift in mindset. As a consultant, you are not just a service provider; you are a business owner, responsible for every aspect of your practice. Embracing this entrepreneurial mindset is crucial for navigating the challenges and opportunities of consulting.

Key Mindset Shifts for New Consultants:

1. **Ownership and Accountability:** As a consultant, you are fully accountable for your success. This means taking ownership of your outcomes, being proactive in seeking clients, and continually refining your skills and services. Unlike traditional employment, where responsibilities are often shared, consulting places the onus on you to drive your business forward.

2. **Embracing Uncertainty:** Consulting involves inherent uncertainties, from variable income to fluctuating client demand. Cultivating a mindset that is comfortable with uncertainty allows you to navigate these challenges with resilience. Embrace uncertainty as an opportunity for growth and innovation rather than a barrier to success.

3. **Proactive Problem-Solving:** In consulting, problem-solving extends beyond client projects to include the business itself. Whether it's finding clients, managing cash flow, or adapting to market changes, being proactive in identifying and solving problems is a critical skill for consultants.

4. **Continuous Learning and Adaptation:** The consulting landscape is dynamic, and staying relevant requires a commitment to continuous learning. Be open to acquiring new skills, exploring emerging trends, and adapting your services to meet evolving client needs. A growth mindset will keep you competitive and positioned for long-term success.

AI Reflection Prompt: *What mindset shifts do I need to make as I transition from being an employee to running my own consulting business, and how can I cultivate an entrepreneurial mindset?*

21.2 INITIAL FINANCIAL PLANNING: SETTING A SOLID FOUNDATION

Financial planning is a cornerstone of a successful transition into consulting. While detailed financial planning will come later, starting with some basic steps can help you build a solid foundation and reduce the financial risks associated with consulting.

Key Financial Considerations for Your Transition:

1. **Build a Financial Buffer:** A financial buffer, or emergency fund, is essential for managing the initial uncertainties of consulting. Aim to save at least three to six months' worth of living expenses to cover periods of low income or unexpected costs. This buffer will provide peace of mind and allow you to focus on building your consulting business without the immediate pressure of income variability.

2. **Assess Your Current Financial Situation:** Take stock of your current financial situation, including your savings, debt, monthly expenses, and any financial commitments. Understanding your financial baseline will help you set realistic income goals and identify areas where you can reduce expenses to support your transition.

3. **Estimate Your Initial Business Expenses:** While consulting generally has lower startup costs compared to other businesses, there are still initial expenses to consider, such as marketing, software tools, professional memberships, and legal or accounting fees. Estimate these costs and factor them into your financial planning.

4. **Plan for Taxes and Benefits:** As a consultant, you will be responsible for managing your own taxes, health insurance, and retirement savings. Set aside a portion of your income for taxes and explore options for health coverage and retirement planning. This proactive approach will help you avoid financial surprises and ensure that your personal and business finances are in good order.

5. **Set Income Milestones:** Establish preliminary income milestones to guide your transition. These milestones might include securing your first client, reaching a target monthly income, or achieving financial stability by a certain date. Setting these benchmarks will help you measure progress and maintain focus during the early stages of consulting.

AI Reflection Prompt: *Based on my current financial situation [insert details], what steps should I take to prepare for the financial realities of consulting, including savings, budgeting, and managing business expenses?*

21.3 SETTING PERSONAL MILESTONES: A ROADMAP FOR YOUR TRANSITION

Creating personal milestones is an effective way to structure your transition into consulting and keep your efforts aligned with your goals. Milestones serve as guideposts, helping you track progress and celebrate achievements along the way.

Steps to Setting Personal Milestones:

1. **Define Your Transition Timeline:** Start by defining your overall timeline for transitioning into consulting. Are you planning to make the shift within three months, six months, or a year? Having a clear timeline will help you prioritise tasks and manage your transition more effectively.
2. **Identify Key Milestones:** Break down your transition timeline into key milestones. Consider milestones that cover different aspects of your transition, including mindset, financial readiness, business setup, and client acquisition.

Examples of Key Milestones:

- **Mindset Milestone:** Completing a mindset shift exercise or attending a workshop on entrepreneurship.
- **Financial Milestone:** Saving a specific amount for your financial buffer or reducing personal expenses by a target percentage.

- **Business Milestone:** Setting up your consulting website, registering your business, or developing your service offerings.
- **Client Milestone:** Securing your first client, completing your first project, or receiving your first testimonial.

3. **Set SMART Milestones:** Ensure that your milestones are SMART: Specific, Measurable, Achievable, Relevant, and Time-bound. For example, instead of setting a vague milestone like "start consulting," set a specific goal such as "secure my first consulting client within three months."

4. **Create a Milestone Tracker:** Use a milestone tracker, such as a spreadsheet, project management tool, or even a simple checklist, to monitor your progress. Regularly update your tracker, celebrate completed milestones, and adjust your plan as needed based on your experiences and learnings.

AI Reflection Prompt: *What key milestones should I set for my transition into consulting, and how can I break them down into manageable, time-bound steps?*

21.4 PREPARING FOR THE TRANSITION: ACTIONABLE STEPS

With your mindset shifts, financial planning, and personal milestones in place, it's time to take actionable steps toward your consulting transition. Here are some initial actions to get you started:

1. **Begin Networking and Building Connections:** Start reaching out to your network to inform them about your transition into consulting. Attend industry events, join professional groups, and actively engage on platforms like LinkedIn. Building connections early on will help you generate leads, gain referrals, and position yourself within your target market.

2. **Develop Your Personal Brand:** Establishing a strong personal brand is crucial for consulting success. Begin by refining your LinkedIn profile, creating a professional website, and crafting a clear and compelling unique value proposition. Your personal

brand should reflect your expertise, values, and the specific problems you solve for clients.

3. **Set Up Basic Business Infrastructure:** Set up the basic infrastructure for your consulting business, including your business name, legal structure, and any necessary registrations or licences. Consider opening a separate business bank account to keep your finances organised and establish a professional invoicing system for managing payments.

4. **Explore Potential Niche Opportunities:** Continue exploring potential niche opportunities that align with your skills and market demand. Conduct market research, test different service offerings, and remain open to refining your focus based on feedback and insights.

5. **Create a Marketing Action Plan:** Develop a basic marketing action plan to start promoting your consulting services. Identify initial marketing channels, such as content creation, social media, or email outreach, and set small, manageable goals for building your visibility and attracting clients.

AI Reflection Prompt: *What are the most important first steps I should take to begin my transition into consulting, including networking, branding, and setting up business infrastructure?*

21.5 EMBRACING FLEXIBILITY AND PATIENCE

As you create your preliminary transition plan, it's important to embrace flexibility and patience. Consulting is a journey, and while a plan provides direction, it's normal for things to evolve along the way. Stay open to adjusting your plan based on new insights, feedback, and experiences.

Tips for Embracing Flexibility and Patience:

- **Expect Iterations:** Your transition plan is not set in stone. Be willing to iterate and refine your approach as you gain more clarity about what works best for you and your consulting business.

- **Practice Self-Compassion:** Transitioning into consulting is a significant change, and it's natural to encounter challenges or feel uncertain at times. Practice self-compassion, acknowledge your efforts, and celebrate the progress you make, no matter how small.
- **Stay Committed to Your Vision:** Keep your long-term vision in mind as you navigate your transition. While the path may have twists and turns, staying committed to your ultimate goals will help you persevere through the ups and downs.

AI Reflection Prompt: *How can I balance having a structured transition plan with the flexibility to adapt based on new insights and opportunities?*

Creating a preliminary transition plan is an essential step in preparing for your move into solo consulting. By focusing on mindset shifts, initial financial planning, and setting personal milestones, you can lay a strong foundation for a successful transition. Remember that your plan is a guide, not a rigid blueprint—be open to adapting it as you gain new insights and experiences.

As you move forward, keep your vision clear, your mindset resilient, and your actions aligned with your goals. With thoughtful preparation and a commitment to your journey, you'll be well-positioned to navigate the transition into consulting with confidence and purpose.

KEY CONCEPTS

A preliminary transition plan provides structure and confidence for moving into consulting. While flexibility is necessary, early planning sets a strong foundation for long-term success.

1. **Shifting Your Mindset: From Employee to Entrepreneur**

Consulting requires a shift from employee thinking to entrepreneurial ownership.

Success depends on accountability, problem-solving, and continuous learning.

Comfort with uncertainty is essential, as income and client flow may fluctuate.

2. **Initial Financial Planning: Setting a Solid Foundation**

Build a Financial Buffer: Aim for 3–6 months of living expenses to manage income variability.

Assess Current Finances: Review savings, debt, and expenses to set realistic financial goals.

Estimate Business Costs: Consider startup expenses such as marketing, legal fees, and tools.

Plan for Taxes and Benefits: Set aside funds for self-employment taxes and research healthcare and retirement options.

Set Income Milestones: Define financial benchmarks to track progress towards sustainability.

3. **Setting Personal Milestones: A Roadmap for Your Transition**

Define Your Timeline: Decide whether to transition in months or years.

Establish Key Milestones: Break goals into mindset, financial, business, and client acquisition targets.

Use SMART Goals: Ensure milestones are Specific, Measurable, Achievable, Relevant, and Time-bound.

Track Progress: Use tools such as spreadsheets or project management apps to monitor milestones.

4. Preparing for the Transition: Actionable Steps

Start Networking Early: Engage with industry contacts, attend events, and build relationships.

Develop Your Personal Brand: Optimise LinkedIn, create a website, and refine your unique value proposition.

Set Up Business Infrastructure: Register your business, open a bank account, and establish invoicing systems.

Explore and Test Your Niche: Conduct market research and refine your consulting focus based on demand.

Create a Basic Marketing Plan: Identify how you will promote your services (e.g., social media, email outreach).

5. Embracing Flexibility and Patience

The transition plan should evolve based on insights and new opportunities.

Iteration is normal—refining the plan based on real-world experiences is key.

Self-compassion is important—progress takes time, and setbacks are learning experiences.

Stay committed to long-term success while remaining adaptable.

EXERCISE: DRAFT YOUR PRELIMINARY TRANSITION PLAN

Step 1: Define Your Transition Timeline. Decide on a realistic timeline for transitioning into consulting. This could be immediate, within the next six months, or over the course of a year. Outline key milestones along this timeline.

Step 2: Identify Core Elements of Your Plan. List the core elements that need to be addressed in your transition plan, such as financial preparation, skill development, marketing, client acquisition, and business setup.

Step 3: Set Personal Milestones. For each core element, set specific, measurable milestones. For example:

- **Financial Preparation:** Save three months' worth of living expenses by [specific date].
- **Skill Development:** Complete a relevant online course by [specific date].
- **Marketing:** Create a LinkedIn profile and start networking by [specific date].

Step 4: Outline Action Steps. Break down each milestone into smaller, actionable steps. Assign a timeframe to each action step to help keep yourself on track.

Step 5: Reflect on Your Transition Plan. Consider how well your transition plan aligns with your overall goals. Are there any areas that feel overwhelming or need further clarification? What support or resources might you need to stay on track?

Step 6: Commit to Initial Actions. Identify the first three actions you will take to begin implementing your transition plan. Set a date for each and commit to getting started.

22: BUILDING CONFIDENCE AND RESILIENCE

E mbarking on a consulting journey requires not only practical skills and preparation but also a strong sense of confidence and resilience.

It is common for new consultants to face fears, imposter syndrome, and external doubts—challenges that can undermine self-assurance and commitment. Building confidence and resilience is essential for navigating these obstacles and sustaining motivation as you transition into consulting.

In this chapter, we explore tips and strategies for building confidence in your decision to consult, handling common fears, overcoming imposter syndrome, and managing external doubts.

22.1 UNDERSTANDING COMMON FEARS AND DOUBTS

As you consider transitioning into consulting, it is normal to experience fears and doubts. Acknowledging these feelings is the first step in addressing them. Common fears among new consultants include:

- **Fear of Failure:** The fear of not succeeding in consulting can be paralyzing. Concerns about finding clients, managing finances, or delivering results can create anxiety and self-doubt.
- **Fear of Financial Instability:** Consulting often comes with income variability, which can trigger fears about financial security and the ability to meet personal or business expenses.
- **Fear of Rejection:** Consulting involves pitching your services and facing potential rejection. The prospect of hearing "no" from clients can be daunting, especially when you are just starting.
- **Fear of the Unknown:** Consulting requires stepping into the unknown, leaving behind the predictability of a traditional job. This uncertainty can lead to fears about navigating new challenges and responsibilities.

Recognising these fears as normal and temporary responses to change can help you manage them more effectively. By taking proactive steps to build confidence and resilience, you can reduce the impact of these fears on your decision-making and actions.

> **AI Reflection Prompt:** *What are the biggest fears about transitioning into consulting, and how can I break them down into manageable concerns with actionable solutions?*

22.2 STRATEGIES FOR BUILDING CONFIDENCE IN CONSULTING

Confidence in your decision to consult—and in your abilities as a consultant—can be developed through intentional strategies and practices. Here are some key approaches to building confidence:

1. Start with Small Wins. Building confidence often starts with achieving small wins that reinforce your abilities and decisions. Rather than immediately aiming for large, high-stakes projects, begin with smaller, manageable tasks that allow you to demonstrate your skills and gain positive feedback.

Examples of Small Wins:

- Completing a successful initial consultation or discovery call with a potential client.
- Receiving positive feedback on a proposal or early project.
- Securing your first client, even if it is for a small project or at a lower rate than your long-term goal, is important.

Each small win serves as a stepping stone, boosting your confidence and reinforcing your belief in your capabilities as a consultant.

2. Reframe Negative Thoughts. Negative self-talk and limiting beliefs can undermine your confidence and contribute to imposter syndrome. Practice reframing these thoughts by challenging their validity and replacing them with more constructive perspectives.

Examples of Reframing:

- Instead of "I'm not experienced enough to be a consultant," reframe to "My unique experiences and skills bring valuable insights to my clients."
- Instead of "What if I fail?" reframe to "Every experience is an opportunity to learn and grow, whether it is successful or not."

By consciously shifting your mindset, you can create a more positive and empowering narrative that supports your confidence.

3. Celebrate Your Progress. Acknowledging and celebrating your progress, no matter how small, is a powerful way to build confidence. Recognise the steps you have taken, the skills you have developed, and the challenges you have overcome along the way.

Ways to Celebrate Progress:

- Keep a success journal where you record achievements, positive feedback, and moments of personal growth.
- Share your wins with a supportive friend, mentor, or

community who can celebrate with you and provide
encouragement.

- Reward yourself for milestones reached, whether it is taking
  time for a favourite activity, treating yourself to something
  special, or simply pausing to reflect on your journey.

4. Focus on Your Unique Value. Confidence comes from knowing and
embracing your unique value proposition—the specific strengths,
skills, and perspectives that set you apart as a consultant. Spend time
identifying your unique value and learning how to articulate it clearly.

Action Steps:

- List your top skills, achievements, and experiences that are
  relevant to your consulting services.
- Develop a clear elevator pitch that communicates your unique
  value to potential clients. Practice delivering it confidently in
  different settings.
- Gather testimonials, case studies, or examples of past successes
  that highlight your impact. These serve as tangible evidence of
  your value and can boost your confidence when shared with
  prospective clients.

5. Build a Supportive Network. Surrounding yourself with a
supportive network of peers, mentors, and like-minded individuals
can provide both practical support and emotional encouragement. A
strong network serves as a source of advice, accountability, and
motivation.

Ways to Build Your Network:

- Join professional associations, online forums, or local meetups
  for consultants in your field. Engaging with a community of
  peers allows you to share experiences, ask questions, and learn
  from others.
- Seek out mentors who can provide guidance, feedback, and
  reassurance as you navigate the early stages of consulting.

Mentors can offer perspectives that help validate your decisions and boost your confidence.

- Connect with fellow consultants who are also starting out. Building relationships with others on a similar journey can create a sense of camaraderie and shared support.

AI Reflection Prompt: *What small wins can I focus on in the early stages of consulting to build confidence and reinforce my belief in my abilities?*

22.3 OVERCOMING IMPOSTER SYNDROME

Imposter syndrome—the feeling that you're not as competent as others perceive you to be—is a common challenge for consultants, especially when transitioning into a new role. Overcoming imposter syndrome involves recognising these feelings and adopting strategies to counteract them.

Tips for Managing Imposter Syndrome:

1. **Acknowledge Your Achievements:** Imposter syndrome often causes you to downplay your accomplishments. Take time to reflect on your achievements, skills, and the positive impact you've had in your previous roles. Acknowledge that your successes are the result of your hard work and abilities, not luck or external factors.

2. **Normalise the Experience:** Understand that imposter syndrome is a common experience, even among highly successful individuals. You're not alone in feeling this way, and it's a natural response to stepping outside your comfort zone. Recognising this can reduce the power of imposter syndrome over your self-perception.

3. **Shift Focus from Perfection to Progress:** Perfectionism can exacerbate imposter syndrome, as it sets unrealistic standards that are impossible to meet. Shift your focus from trying to be perfect to making progress and delivering value. Remember that your clients are seeking solutions, not perfection, and that your expertise is valuable even if you're still learning.

4. **Take Action Despite Self-Doubt:** Confidence often follows action. Taking steps forward, even when you feel uncertain, can help diminish imposter syndrome over time. Each successful action, no matter how small, builds evidence that you are capable and competent.

   AI Reflection Prompt: *How can I use past successes (solved problems or delivered results) to counter imposter syndrome in consulting?*

22.4 HANDLING EXTERNAL DOUBTS AND CRITICISM

In addition to internal doubts, new consultants may encounter scepticism or criticism from others—whether it is from friends, family, or even potential clients. Handling external doubts with confidence and resilience is key to maintaining your commitment to consulting.

Strategies for Managing External Doubts:

1. **Stay Grounded in Your Decision:** Remind yourself of the reasons why you chose consulting and the preparation you've put into your transition. Stay connected to your vision and values, letting them anchor you when faced with external doubts.
2. **Seek Constructive Feedback:** Not all criticism is negative. Constructive feedback can provide valuable insights for improvement. Be open to feedback that is specific, actionable, and intended to help you grow. Use it as an opportunity to refine your approach and build resilience.
3. **Set Boundaries with Naysayers:** While some criticism is helpful, not all opinions are constructive or relevant. Set boundaries with individuals whose doubts are not aligned with your goals or who consistently undermine your confidence. Surround yourself with those who support and believe in your journey.
4. **Use Doubts as Fuel for Growth:** Use external doubts as motivation to prove to yourself that you are capable of succeeding. Rather than internalising negative feedback,

channel it into determination and action. Let it drive you to further develop your skills, deliver exceptional value, and achieve your consulting goals.

AI Reflection Prompt: *How can I maintain confidence in my decision to be a consultant when faced with scepticism from friends, family, or potential clients?*

22.5 CULTIVATING RESILIENCE FOR THE LONG HAUL

Resilience is the capacity to recover from setbacks, adapt to change, and keep moving forward in the face of challenges. Cultivating resilience is essential for sustaining your consulting journey over the long term.

Key Practices for Building Resilience:

1. **Embrace Challenges as Learning Opportunities:** View challenges and setbacks as opportunities for learning and growth. Reflect on what went wrong, what you can improve, and how you can apply these lessons in the future. A resilient mindset sees failure not as a stopping point but as a stepping stone.

2. **Practice Self-Compassion:** Treat yourself with the same kindness and understanding you would offer to a friend. Recognise that consulting is a journey with highs and lows, and it's okay to have moments of doubt or difficulty. Self-compassion fosters resilience by reducing the impact of self-criticism.

3. **Stay Focused on Your Long-Term Vision:** Keep your long-term vision in mind, especially during challenging times. Reconnect with your goals, values, and the impact you want to make through consulting. This focus helps maintain your motivation and commitment, even when faced with obstacles.

4. **Prioritise Well-Being and Balance:** Resilience is closely tied to your overall well-being. Prioritise self-care, maintain a healthy work-life balance, and make time for activities that recharge

and nourish you. Taking care of your physical, mental, and emotional health strengthens your capacity to handle stress and setbacks.

Building confidence and resilience is a critical aspect of transitioning into solo consulting. By recognising and addressing common fears, reframing negative thoughts, and embracing a supportive network, you can cultivate the self-assurance needed to succeed in consulting. Overcoming imposter syndrome and managing external doubts are ongoing processes, but with intentional strategies and a growth-oriented mindset, you can navigate these challenges with confidence.

Resilience empowers you to adapt, learn, and persevere through the ups and downs of consulting. By viewing challenges as opportunities and staying focused on your long-term vision, you can sustain your motivation and thrive in your consulting journey. Remember, confidence is not the absence of doubt—it's the willingness to take action despite it. Trust in your abilities, stay committed to your path, and approach each step of your consulting career with resilience and optimism.

> **AI Reflection Prompt:** *What personal resilience strategies (such as self-care, networking, or mindset shifts) can I develop to stay motivated and navigate setbacks in consulting?*

KEY CONCEPTS

Confidence and resilience are essential for navigating the challenges of consulting. By addressing fears, reframing doubts, and building a strong mindset, you can sustain motivation and achieve success.

1. Understanding Common Fears and Doubts

Fear of Failure: Worries about client acquisition, financial stability, and project success.

Fear of Financial Instability: Concerns about income variability and managing expenses.

Fear of Rejection: Anxiety about pitching services and facing potential rejection.

Fear of the Unknown: Uncertainty about transitioning from a structured job to independent consulting.

2. Strategies for Building Confidence in Consulting

Start with Small Wins: Gain confidence through early, manageable successes.

Reframe Negative Thoughts: Shift from self-doubt to a constructive, empowered mindset.

Celebrate Progress: Track achievements and reflect on growth to reinforce self-belief.

Focus on Unique Value: Define and articulate your expertise and differentiation.

Build a Supportive Network: Engage with mentors, peers, and like-minded professionals for encouragement.

3. Overcoming Imposter Syndrome

Acknowledge Your Achievements: Recognise your past successes and strengths.

Normalise the Experience: Understand that imposter syndrome is common and does not reflect reality.

Shift from Perfection to Progress: Focus on delivering value rather than achieving perfection.

Take Action Despite Doubt: Confidence grows through consistent effort and learning.

4. Handling External Doubts and Criticism

Stay Grounded in Your Decision: Reaffirm why consulting aligns with your career and life goals.

Seek Constructive Feedback: Use external input to improve, not as a source of discouragement.

Set Boundaries with Naysayers: Limit exposure to negativity and focus on supportive influences.

Use Doubts as Motivation: Channel scepticism into determination and skill development.

5. **Cultivating Resilience for the Long Haul**

Embrace Challenges as Learning Opportunities: View setbacks as part of the growth process.

Practice Self-Compassion: Acknowledge struggles without harsh self-judgement.

Stay Focused on Your Long-Term Vision: Keep sight of why you started and what success looks like.

Prioritise Well-Being and Balance: Maintain work-life integration to sustain motivation and performance.

EXERCISE: CONFIDENCE AND RESILIENCE BUILDING PLAN

Step 1: Identify Key Doubts or Fears. List your top doubts, fears, or challenges about consulting. Be specific—whether it's fear of financial instability, self-doubt about your skills, or concern about finding clients.

Step 2: Reframe Negative Thoughts. For each doubt or fear, write down a positive reframe. For example, if you fear not finding clients, reframe it as: "I have a valuable skill set and a network I can leverage to find my first clients."

Step 3: Develop Confidence-Building Strategies. Identify specific strategies to build confidence in each area of doubt. These might include:

- **Skill Mastery:** Commit to ongoing learning and practice.
- **Networking:** Schedule regular networking activities to build connections.
- **Small Wins:** Set small, achievable goals to build momentum and celebrate successes.

Step 4: Create a Resilience Toolkit. Develop a toolkit of resilience strategies to use when facing setbacks. Include practices such as journaling, mindfulness, exercise, seeking feedback, or reaching out to mentors.

Step 5: Reflect on Your Toolkit. Consider how these strategies make you feel about your readiness for consulting. What additional support or adjustments might enhance your confidence and resilience?

Step 6: Commit to Regular Practice. Choose one confidence-building and one resilience strategy to start practising regularly. Set a schedule for these practices, such as weekly reflections or daily affirmations, to integrate them into your routine.

23: LEVERAGING YOUR NETWORK AND EXISTING RESOURCES

As you transition into solo consulting, one of your most valuable assets is your existing professional network, along with the skills and resources you have accumulated throughout your career.

Leveraging these connections and capabilities can significantly ease your transition, reduce the initial learning curve, and provide a strong foundation for your consulting practice.

This chapter highlights the importance of utilising your professional network, existing skills, and available resources to support your move into consulting and offer strategies for making the most of what you already have.

23.1 THE POWER OF YOUR PROFESSIONAL NETWORK

Your professional network is an invaluable resource as you embark on your consulting journey. It consists of colleagues, former managers, clients, industry peers, and others with whom you have interacted throughout the course of your career. These connections can provide referrals, advice, insights, and even potential clients, making them a crucial component of your transition strategy.

Ways to Leverage Your Network:

1. **Reach Out to Existing Contacts**. Start by reaching out to your existing contacts to inform them of your transition into consulting. Personal connections are often the most effective source of initial opportunities and referrals.

   - **Inform Your Network:** Send a personalised message or email to your professional network announcing your new consulting venture. Share the services you offer, your unique value proposition, and how you can help potential clients.
   - **Ask for Referrals:** Don't hesitate to ask for referrals or introductions to individuals or organisations that might need your services. Be specific about the types of clients or industries you are targeting to make it easier for your contacts to connect you with the right opportunities.
   - **Offer Value First:** Approach your network with a mindset of giving rather than just taking. Offer your help, share useful resources, or provide a complimentary consultation to demonstrate your expertise and build goodwill.

2. **Engage on LinkedIn and Social Media**. LinkedIn and other professional social media platforms are powerful tools for networking and showcasing your consulting services. Use these platforms to stay connected, share content, and position yourself as an expert in your field.

   - **Optimise Your Profile:** Ensure your LinkedIn profile is up to date, professional, and clearly communicates your consulting services. Highlight your skills, experiences, and any case studies or testimonials that demonstrate your value.
   - **Share Valuable Content:** Regularly share articles, insights, and updates related to your consulting niche. Engaging content positions you as a thought leader and keeps you top of mind with your network.

- **Join Industry Groups:** Participate in LinkedIn groups or online forums related to your industry or consulting niche. Engage in discussions, answer questions, and contribute your expertise to build connections and visibility.

3. **Attend Networking Events and Industry Conferences.** In-person or virtual networking events and industry conferences offer excellent opportunities to expand your network and meet potential clients.

- **Choose Relevant Events:** Focus on events that attract your target audience or industry peers. This increases the likelihood of meeting individuals who are interested in your consulting services.
- **Prepare Your Elevator Pitch:** Have a concise and compelling elevator pitch ready that clearly explains who you are, what you do, and how you can help. Practice delivering it confidently to make a strong impression.
- **Follow Up Promptly:** After networking events, follow up with the people you met. Send a personalised message, connect on LinkedIn, and continue the conversation to build a meaningful relationship.

4. **Reconnect with Past Colleagues and Clients.** Your former colleagues and clients already know your capabilities and can be a great source of early consulting work or referrals.

- **Reach Out with a Purpose:** Contact former colleagues and clients with a clear intention, such as catching up, discussing potential collaboration, or seeking their insights on your transition into consulting.
- **Leverage Past Successes:** Highlight specific successes or projects you worked on together that are relevant to your consulting services. Remind them of the value you provided and how your expertise can benefit them or their network now.

AI Reflection Prompt: *How will I identify who in my existing network could provide valuable advice, referrals, or collaboration opportunities for my consulting business?*

23.2 UTILISING YOUR EXISTING SKILLS AND EXPERTISE

Your existing skills and expertise are the foundation of your consulting practice. Leveraging what you already know can help you deliver value from day one and reduce the time it takes to establish credibility in the consulting market.

Strategies for Leveraging Your Skills:

1. **Identify Your Core Competencies**. Take stock of your core competencies and how they align with your consulting goals. Consider the specific skills, knowledge, and experiences that set you apart and can address your clients' needs.

   - **Conduct a Skills Inventory:** List your technical skills, industry expertise, problem-solving abilities, and any unique approaches you've developed in your career. Reflect on which skills are most relevant and marketable in your consulting niche.
   - **Highlight Transferable Skills:** Don't overlook transferable skills such as project management, communication, and strategic thinking. These skills are highly valuable in consulting and can be applied across various industries and client projects.

2. **Leverage Industry Experience and Insights**. Your industry experience provides you with a unique perspective and understanding of the challenges, trends, and opportunities within your target market.

   - **Showcase Industry Expertise:** Use your industry insights to differentiate yourself from competitors. Highlight your experience in specific sectors, your knowledge of industry regulations, and your familiarity with common pain points that clients face.

- **Develop Niche-Specific Content:** Create content that reflects your industry expertise, such as blog posts, white papers, or webinars. Sharing your knowledge positions you as a trusted advisor and attracts clients who value your specialised insights.

3. **Utilise Your Problem-Solving Experience**. Consulting is fundamentally about solving problems for clients. Reflect on past experiences where you've successfully identified and addressed complex challenges.

- **Create Case Studies:** Develop case studies that outline specific problems you've solved in your career. Detail the situation, your approach, and the results achieved. Case studies serve as powerful proof of your ability to deliver value and can be used in your marketing materials.
- **Emphasise Results:** Focus on the outcomes you've delivered, such as cost savings, process improvements, or enhanced performance. Quantifiable results provide compelling evidence of your impact and can help build trust with potential clients.

AI Reflection Prompt: *How can I best leverage my core skills and past experiences to differentiate myself as a consultant and attract potential clients?*

23.3 LEVERAGING OTHER RESOURCES TO SUPPORT YOUR TRANSITION

Beyond your network and skills, there are additional resources you can leverage to support your transition into consulting. These resources can provide practical assistance, streamline your processes, and enhance your professional presence.

Resources to Leverage:

1. **Existing Tools and Software**. Utilise existing tools and software that you are familiar with to manage your consulting business. This can include project management tools, accounting software, CRM systems, and communication platforms.

   - **Optimise Familiar Tools:** Stick with tools you already know well, as this reduces the time spent on learning new systems and allows you to focus on delivering client value.
   - **Explore Free or Low-Cost Options:** There are numerous free or low-cost tools available that can help you manage your consulting business efficiently. Look for solutions that offer the functionality you need without a significant upfront investment.

2. **Professional Associations and Certifications**. Professional associations and certifications can provide credibility, networking opportunities, and access to industry resources that support your consulting practice.

   - **Join Relevant Associations:** Becoming a member of industry-specific associations can enhance your professional standing, provide access to member directories, and offer opportunities for professional development.
   - **Pursue Certifications:** Relevant certifications can validate your expertise and set you apart in your niche. Consider certifications that are recognised and valued by your target clients.

3. **Educational and Learning Resources**. Continuous learning is essential for staying competitive in consulting. Leverage existing educational resources, such as online courses, webinars, and industry publications, to keep your skills up-to-date and expand your knowledge.

- **Use Free Learning Platforms:** Platforms like Coursera, edX, and LinkedIn Learning offer a wide range of courses on consulting skills, business management, and industry-specific topics. Many of these courses are available for free or at a low cost.
- **Stay Informed with Industry News:** Regularly read industry news, follow thought leaders, and subscribe to relevant newsletters. Staying informed helps you anticipate trends, identify new opportunities, and position yourself as a knowledgeable consultant.

AI Reflection Prompt: *What existing tools or learning resources can I use to streamline my transition into consulting and enhance my credibility?*

23.4 REDUCING THE INITIAL LEARNING CURVE

Leveraging your network, skills, and resources effectively can significantly reduce the initial learning curve associated with starting a consulting business. Here are some additional tips to ease your transition:

1. **Focus on What You Know Best**. Start by offering services in areas where you already have deep expertise and confidence. This allows you to deliver high-quality work with minimal learning time, building your reputation and client base more quickly.
2. **Seek Guidance from Experienced Consultants**. Don't hesitate to seek advice from experienced consultants who can share their insights and lessons learned. Mentors, peers, or consultants in your network can provide practical guidance that accelerates your learning and helps you avoid common pitfalls.
3. **Leverage Templates and Frameworks.** Use existing templates, frameworks, and methodologies that are proven in your field. Whether it's a project management template, a consulting proposal format, or a client onboarding process,

leveraging established tools can save time and ensure consistency.

4. **Start with a Pilot Project**. Consider starting with a pilot project or a trial run of your services. This allows you to test your consulting approach, gather feedback, and refine your offerings without the pressure of a full-scale launch. Use the insights gained from the pilot to improve your processes and build confidence.

AI Reflection Prompt: *What steps can I take to shorten my learning curve in consulting?*

Leveraging your existing professional network, skills, and resources is a strategic way to ease your transition into consulting and reduce the initial learning curve. By tapping into what you already have, you can build a strong foundation for your consulting practice, connect with potential clients, and demonstrate your value from the outset.

You don't have to start from scratch; your career has already equipped you with valuable assets that can support your consulting journey. Embrace these resources, stay connected to your network, and continue to build on your expertise as you move forward. With the right mindset and a proactive approach, you will be well-positioned to succeed in your transition into consulting.

KEY CONCEPTS

Leveraging your network, skills, and available resources accelerates your transition into consulting. You don't need to start from scratch; use your career assets to gain early momentum. Proactively engaging with your network and maximising existing tools can reduce the challenges of starting out.

1. The Power of Your Professional Network

Your network—colleagues, managers, and industry peers—can provide referrals, insights, and support.

Ways to leverage your network:

- Reach out to existing contacts and inform them about your consulting services.
- Engage actively on LinkedIn and social media to increase visibility.
- Attend networking events, industry conferences, and professional meet-ups.
- Reconnect with past colleagues and clients who already know your strengths.

2. Utilising Your Existing Skills and Expertise

Identify your core competencies that are most valuable in consulting.

Highlight industry experience and insights to differentiate yourself.

Use problem-solving experiences from past roles to demonstrate expertise.

Develop case studies or success stories to showcase your impact.

3. Leveraging Other Resources to Support Your Transition

Use familiar tools and software for project management, accounting, and client communication.

Join professional associations for networking, industry credibility, and continued learning.

Invest in certifications or relevant training to strengthen your expertise.

Stay updated on industry trends through online courses, webinars, and publications.

4. Reducing the Initial Learning Curve

Focus on services that align with your existing expertise to gain traction quickly.

Seek advice from experienced consultants and mentors to avoid common pitfalls.

Use templates and established frameworks to streamline processes.

Start with a pilot project to refine your approach before a full-scale launch.

EXERCISE: NETWORK AND RESOURCE MAPPING

Step 1: Map Your Network. Create a visual map of your existing network, including past colleagues, industry contacts, mentors, professional groups, and online communities. Highlight individuals who may offer valuable support, advice, or referrals.

Step 2: Identify Key Skills and Resources. List your key skills and any existing resources (such as software, tools, templates, or professional memberships) that you can leverage in your consulting business.

Step 3: Plan Your Outreach. Select 5-10 individuals from your network whom you will approach for advice, feedback, or potential collaboration. Draft a brief outreach message for each, clearly stating your purpose and what you are seeking.

Step 4: Develop a Resource Utilisation Plan. For each skill or resource, outline how you will use it in your consulting business. For example:

- **Skill:** Use your project management expertise to streamline client projects.
- **Resource:** Utilise your existing CRM software to manage client relationships.

Step 5: Reflect on Your Network and Resources. Assess the strength of your network and resources. How can these connections and tools help ease your transition into consulting? Are there any gaps that need to be filled?

Step 6: Take Action on Outreach and Utilisation. Commit to reaching out to at least three contacts this week and to utilising one key resource in a specific aspect of your consulting business setup.

24: STAYING CONNECTED TO YOUR WHY

As you embark on your consulting journey, it is crucial to stay connected to the deeper motivations behind your decision to pursue this path.

Your "why"—the core reasons that inspired you to explore solo consulting—serves as a powerful guide and anchor through the uncertainties, challenges, and inevitable ups and downs that come with building a consulting practice.

In this chapter, we emphasise the importance of staying connected to your why and offer strategies for using your motivations as a source of resilience, direction, and inspiration.

24.1 UNDERSTANDING THE POWER OF YOUR WHY

Your why is more than just a set of goals; it is the underlying purpose that drives your actions and decisions. It encompasses your values, passions, and the impact you want to make through your work. Staying connected to your why helps you maintain focus, navigate obstacles, and make decisions that are aligned with your true self.

Why Staying Connected to Your Why Matters:

- **Provides Clarity and Direction:** Your why acts as a compass, guiding your choices and helping you prioritise actions that align with your long-term vision.
- **Builds Resilience:** During challenging times, your why serves as a reminder of why you started and what you are working toward, helping you stay motivated and resilient.
- **Inspires Commitment:** Staying connected to your why reinforces your commitment to your consulting journey, even when faced with setbacks or doubts.
- **Fosters Authenticity:** When your actions are aligned with your why, you operate from a place of authenticity, which resonates with clients and enhances your credibility as a consultant.

AI Reflection Prompt: *How can I clearly define and articulate my "why" for pursuing consulting, and how will it help me stay focused and resilient throughout my journey?*

24.2 IDENTIFYING AND ARTICULATING YOUR WHY

Before you can stay connected to your why, it is important to clearly identify and articulate it. Reflect on the motivations that led you to consider consulting and the values that are most important to you.

Steps to Identify Your Why:

1. **Reflect on Your Motivations**. Consider the key motivations that drew you to consulting. Reflect on both the personal and professional aspects of your decision.

   Questions to Explore:
   What excites me about the idea of consulting?
   What personal or professional needs does consulting fulfil for me?
   How does consulting align with my values and long-term goals?
   Write down your reflections to capture the essence of your why.

Be specific and detailed; the more clearly you can articulate your motivations, the stronger your connection to them will be.

2. **Define the Impact You Want to Make**. Consider the impact you wish to achieve through your consulting work. This may relate to the clients you serve, the problems you solve, or the broader change you hope to contribute to.

   Questions to Explore:
   What difference do I want to make through consulting?
   Who do I want to help, and how can my skills create value for them?
   What legacy or contribution do I hope to achieve in my career?
   Defining the impact you want to make provides a sense of purpose that transcends financial goals or business success, grounding your consulting practice in something meaningful.

3. **Create a Personal Why Statement**. Summarise your reflections into a personal why statement. This statement should encapsulate your core motivations and the impact you aim to achieve.

   Example of a Why Statement: "My why is to empower small businesses to leverage technology for growth, enabling them to compete effectively and thrive in their industries. I am driven by a passion for innovation, a commitment to excellence, and a desire to make a positive difference in the lives of entre-preneurs."

Keep your why statement visible—post it in your workspace, include it in your planning materials, or use it as a daily affirmation. This serves as a constant reminder of your purpose and keeps you aligned with your core motivations.

AI Reflection Prompt: *How can I craft a clear why statement that reflects my core purpose?*

24.3 USING YOUR WHY AS A GUIDE THROUGH CHALLENGES

Challenges are an inevitable part of any consulting journey, but staying connected to your why can provide the strength and clarity needed to navigate them. Here are strategies for using your why as a guide when facing uncertainties or setbacks:

1. **Revisit Your Why During Difficult Times**. When you encounter challenges, take a moment to revisit your why. Remind yourself of the reasons you chose this path and the goals you are working towards.

   Action Steps:

   - Re-read your why statement and reflect on its significance.
   - Journaling can be a helpful tool—write about the current challenge, how it relates to your why, and any insights you gain from reconnecting with your purpose.
   - Consider how your why can help you reframe the challenge as an opportunity for growth or as a necessary step towards your larger goals.

2. **Align Decisions with Your Why**. Use your why as a filter for decision-making. When faced with choices—whether it's taking on a new client, adjusting your services, or making strategic business decisions—ask yourself how each option aligns with your why.

   Questions to Guide Decisions:

   - Does this decision support my why or move me closer to my goals?
   - How does this choice align with my values and the impact I want to make?
   - Will this decision help me stay true to my authentic self as a consultant?

Aligning your decisions with your why ensures that your consulting practice remains focused and authentic, even as you adapt to changing circumstances.

3. **Use Your Why as a Motivation Boost**. Motivation naturally fluctuates, especially when working independently as a consultant. Your why can serve as a powerful motivator during times of low energy or self-doubt.

   Ways to Boost Motivation:

   - Visualise the outcomes of your work and the positive impact it will have on your clients or the broader community.
   - Create a vision board or use images that represent your why and the goals you are striving for. Visual representations can make your motivations feel more tangible and inspiring.
   - Share your why with others—talking about your purpose with friends, mentors, or even clients can reignite your passion and remind you of the bigger picture.

   AI Reflection Prompt: *When I encounter challenges in consulting, how can I use my why to reframe obstacles as opportunities and maintain motivation?*

24.4 STAYING GROUNDED IN YOUR WHY AMID EXTERNAL PRESSURES

External pressures, such as market demands, client expectations, or financial stress, can sometimes pull you away from your core motivations. Staying grounded in your why helps you maintain your direction and resist the temptation to compromise your values.

Strategies for Staying Grounded:

1. **Set Boundaries That Reflect Your Why**. Establishing boundaries is essential for maintaining alignment with your why. This includes setting limits on the types of clients or projects you take on, the hours you work, or the ways you engage with clients.

Examples of Boundaries:

- Declining projects that don't align with your values or expertise, even if they offer financial incentives.
- Setting working hours that support your desired work-life balance, in line with your personal why.
- Communicating clearly with clients about your approach and expectations to ensure mutual alignment.

By setting boundaries that reflect your why, you protect the integrity of your consulting practice and maintain a sense of fulfilment in your work.

2. **Reassess and Realign Regularly**. Periodically reassess your consulting practice to ensure it remains aligned with your why. Regular reflection allows you to make adjustments as needed and stay true to your motivations.

Regular Check-Ins:

- Schedule regular check-ins, such as quarterly reviews, during which you assess your progress, revisit your why, and make any necessary adjustments to your approach or goals.
- Use these check-ins to celebrate successes, acknowledge challenges, and refocus on what is most important to you.

Continuous reassessment keeps your consulting journey dynamic and aligned with your evolving goals and values.

3. **Surround Yourself with Supportive Influences.** The people you surround yourself with can significantly impact your ability to stay connected to your why. Seek out individuals who support and believe in your journey, encouraging you to remain true to your motivations.

Building a Supportive Network:

- Engage with mentors, peers, or communities that share similar values and can provide encouragement, guidance, and accountability.
- Limit exposure to negative influences or individuals who consistently undermine your confidence or distract you from your why.

A supportive network reinforces your commitment to your consulting path and helps you remain focused on your purpose.

AI Reflection Prompt: *How can I set boundaries and make decisions that align with my why, even when faced with financial pressures, market demands, or external expectations?*

24.5 CELEBRATING AND REFLECTING ON YOUR WHY

Staying connected to your why is not just about overcoming challenges; it is also about celebrating the alignment and fulfilment that come from pursuing work that resonates with your true self. Take time to reflect on the moments when your consulting practice aligns with your why and the positive impact you are making.

Ways to Celebrate Your Why:

- **Reflect on Your Impact:** Regularly consider the impact you are having through your consulting work. Acknowledge the ways in which you are helping clients, solving meaningful problems, and contributing to your broader goals.
- **Celebrate Milestones:** Celebrate milestones that reflect your why, such as completing a project that aligns with your values, receiving feedback that validates your purpose, or achieving a goal driven by your core motivations.
- **Share Your Journey:** Share your journey and the role of your why with others. Whether through writing, speaking, or casual

conversations, sharing your story can inspire others and deepen your own connection to your motivations.

Staying connected to your why is a powerful strategy for navigating the consulting journey with purpose, resilience, and authenticity. Your why serves as a guiding light, helping you focus on what matters most, overcome challenges, and make decisions that align with your values and goals.

By regularly revisiting and reflecting on your why, you can maintain the passion and commitment needed to succeed in consulting.

Embrace your motivations, let them inspire your actions, and allow your why to be the anchor that grounds you through every step of your consulting career.

When your work is aligned with your true self, you not only build a successful consulting practice but also create a fulfilling and meaningful professional journey.

AI Reflection Prompt: *How can I regularly reflect on and celebrate my why, ensuring that my consulting work remains meaningful and fulfilling?*

KEY CONCEPTS

Staying connected to your why strengthens motivation, resilience, and fulfilment in consulting. Your why acts as an anchor, helping you navigate challenges, make aligned decisions, and maintain passion for your work.

1. Understanding the Power of Your Why

Your "why" is the core motivation that drives your decision to pursue consulting. It provides **clarity and direction**, keeping your choices aligned with long-term goals.

Staying connected to your why **builds resilience**, helping you overcome challenges. A clear why **inspires commitment**, keeping you motivated despite setbacks.

Operating from your why fosters **authenticity**, making your consulting practice more meaningful and impactful.

2. Identifying and Articulating Your Why

Reflect on your motivations: Consider what excites you about consulting and what personal or professional needs it fulfils.

Define the impact you want to make: Who do you want to help, and what difference do you want to create?

Create a personal why statement: A clear, written statement that summarises your core motivation and the value you aim to provide.

3. Using Your Why as a Guide Through Challenges

Revisit your why during difficult times: Reflecting on your motivations can help you push through challenges.

Align decisions with your why: When facing choices, ask whether they support your deeper purpose.

Use your why as a motivation boost: Visual reminders, journaling, or sharing your why with others can reignite passion and drive.

4. Staying Grounded in Your Why Amid External Pressures

Set boundaries that reflect your why: Ensure your projects, clients, and work structure align with your values.

Reassess and realign regularly: Schedule periodic check-ins to ensure your consulting journey remains aligned with your motivations.

Surround yourself with supportive influences: Engage with mentors, peers, and communities that reinforce your vision.

5. Celebrating and Reflecting on Your Why

Reflect on your impact: Regularly acknowledge how your work aligns with your purpose.

Celebrate milestones: Recognise achievements that bring you closer to fulfilling your why.

Share your journey: Talking about your motivations can deepen your connection to your why and inspire others.

EXERCISE: STAYING CONNECTED TO YOUR WHY

Step 1: Write Your Why Statement. Reflect on and write down your core motivation for pursuing consulting. Be specific about what drives you, whether it is the desire for independence, passion for helping others, or the pursuit of a particular professional goal.

Step 2: Create a Visual Representation. Create a visual representation of your 'why'. This could be a vision board, a simple sketch, or even a digital collage that includes images, words, or symbols that represent your motivation.

Step 3: Identify Alignment Actions. List actions you can take that align with your 'why'. For example, if your 'why' is to help businesses grow, focus on offering services that directly support this goal, such as strategic planning or process improvement.

Step 4: Plan Regular Check-Ins. Schedule regular check-ins (weekly or monthly) to revisit your 'why' and assess how your consulting activities align with it. Use these check-ins to adjust your actions and stay on track with your core motivation.

Step 5: Reflect on Staying Connected. Reflect on how staying connected to your 'why' can help you navigate challenges and maintain motivation. What reminders or rituals can you establish to keep your 'why' front and centre?

Step 6: Share Your Why. Consider sharing your 'why' with a mentor, peer, or supportive friend who can help you stay accountable. Sharing your motivation can reinforce your commitment and provide encouragement along the way.

25: LOOKING AHEAD: WHAT'S NEXT AFTER THE DECISION

Deciding to pursue solo consulting is a significant milestone, marking the beginning of an exciting and transformative journey.

By now, you have explored your motivations, assessed your readiness, weighed the pros and cons, and made a thoughtful decision about whether consulting is the right path for you. As you take this important step forward, it's natural to wonder what comes next.

This chapter offers a brief introduction to what you can expect after making your decision and sets the stage for the next phase of your consulting journey—launching and growing your consulting business.

25.1 EMBRACING YOUR DECISION TO PURSUE CONSULTING

First and foremost, take a moment to acknowledge the decision you have made. Whether you have chosen to dive into consulting full-time, start part-time, or take a gradual approach, embracing your choice with confidence is essential. The clarity you have gained through this decision-making process will serve as a strong foundation for the steps ahead.

Key Actions to Embrace Your Decision:

- **Commit Fully:** Once you have decided to pursue consulting, commit fully to your path. This commitment involves not only practical actions but also a mindset shift that embraces consulting as a central part of your professional identity.
- **Reflect on Your Journey:** Reflect on the process you have gone through to reach this decision. Recognise the growth, insights, and self-awareness you have developed along the way.
- **Set Intentions:** Set clear intentions for the next phase of your consulting journey. Consider what you hope to achieve, the impact you want to make, and the values you want to uphold as you move forward.

AI Reflection Prompt: *How can I fully commit to my decision to pursue consulting, and what intentions can I set to guide my actions and maintain focus on my long-term goals?*

25.2 THE NEXT STEPS: FROM DECISION TO ACTION

After deciding to pursue consulting, the next phase involves turning your decision into action. This phase is about laying the groundwork for your consulting business, establishing your presence in the market, and starting to attract clients. While this book has focused on helping you make an informed decision, the next book in this series will delve into the practical steps of launching and growing your consulting business.

Key Areas to Focus on After Your Decision:

1. **Developing a Comprehensive Business Plan**. A comprehensive business plan is your roadmap for success. It outlines your vision, services, target market, pricing strategy, marketing plan, and financial projections. Crafting a business plan helps you clarify your goals, anticipate challenges, and make informed decisions as you launch your consulting practice.

What to Expect: The next book will guide you through the essential elements of creating a business plan, including defining your niche, setting goals, and developing a strategy to achieve them.

2. **Setting Up Your Consulting Business.** Setting up your consulting business involves more than just registering a business name. It includes establishing your brand, creating a professional online presence, setting up financial and operational systems, and ensuring you have the legal and administrative aspects covered.

What to Expect: You'll learn about the practical steps for setting up your consulting business, from choosing a business structure to creating a compelling brand identity and establishing effective business operations.

3. **Marketing and Client Acquisition.** Marketing and client acquisition are critical components of a successful consulting business. Attracting the right clients, building a strong pipeline, and converting prospects into paying clients require ongoing efforts and a strategic approach.

What to Expect: The next book will delve into strategies for marketing your consulting services, including leveraging your network, creating compelling content, utilising digital marketing, and building a referral system to attract and retain clients.

4. **Delivering Value and Building Client Relationships.** Delivering exceptional value to your clients is at the heart of consulting. Building strong client relationships, managing projects effectively, and continuously improving your service delivery are key to sustaining and growing your business.

What to Expect: You'll explore best practices for managing client relationships, delivering high-quality work, and creating repeat business opportunities through exceptional service and client satisfaction.

5. **Managing Finances and Scaling Your Business.** Financial management is crucial for maintaining a healthy consulting business. Understanding cash flow, setting financial goals, managing expenses, and planning for growth are all part of building a sustainable consulting practice.

What to Expect: The next book will provide insights into financial management for consultants, including budgeting, pricing strategies, managing taxes, and scaling your business over time.

> **AI Reflection Prompt:** *What immediate next steps should I take to begin my consulting journey, and how can I prioritise key areas such as business setup, marketing, and client acquisition?*

25.3 PREPARING FOR THE JOURNEY AHEAD

As you prepare for the journey ahead, it's important to remain flexible and open to learning. Consulting is a dynamic and evolving field, and the ability to adapt, pivot, and continuously refine your approach will be key to your long-term success.

Mindset and Preparation Tips:

- **Embrace Continuous Learning:** Stay curious and committed to learning. Whether it involves new industry trends, emerging technologies, or client feedback, continuous learning will keep you ahead of the curve and enhance your consulting offerings.
- **Cultivate a Growth Mindset:** A growth mindset—the belief that your abilities and skills can be developed through dedication and effort—will help you navigate challenges, embrace new opportunities, and approach your consulting journey with resilience.
- **Celebrate Your Progress:** As you take steps towards launching and growing your consulting business, remember to celebrate your progress. Recognise the milestones you achieve, no matter how small, and use them as motivation to keep moving forward.

Deciding to pursue consulting is a bold and empowering choice, marking the beginning of an exciting new chapter in your professional life. While this book has provided the guidance needed to make an informed decision, the journey of consulting is just beginning. The next steps involve translating your decision into action—planning, setting up your business, acquiring clients, and delivering exceptional value.

As you move forward, stay connected to your 'why', leverage the resources and skills you already possess, and approach each step with confidence and commitment. The next book will guide you through the practical aspects of launching and growing your consulting business, equipping you with the tools and strategies needed to thrive.

Your consulting journey is uniquely yours, and with the right mindset, preparation, and support, you have the potential to build a successful, fulfilling, and impactful consulting practice.

Welcome to the start of an exciting adventure—your next chapter awaits.

> **AI Reflection Prompt:** *How can I cultivate a growth mindset and embrace continuous learning to adapt, refine, and grow my consulting practice over time?*

KEY CONCEPTS

Deciding to pursue consulting is only the beginning; the next phase involves **taking action** and **laying a strong foundation** for success. The consulting journey requires continuous learning, adaptability, and a commitment to long-term growth.

1. Embracing Your Decision to Pursue Consulting

Acknowledge the significance of your decision and commit fully to your new path.

Reflect on your journey and recognise the growth, insights, and clarity you have gained.

Set clear **intentions** for what you hope to achieve in your consulting career.

2. The Next Steps: From Decision to Action

Develop a Comprehensive Business Plan: Define your niche, services, pricing, marketing plan, and financial projections.

Set Up Your Consulting Business: Establish the legal, operational, and branding elements for your firm.

Marketing and Client Acquisition: Build a strong online presence, leverage your network, and create a strategy for attracting clients.

Delivering Value and Building Client Relationships: Focus on high-quality service, strong communication, and ongoing client satisfaction.

Managing Finances and Scaling Your Business: Plan for budgeting, pricing, taxes, and long-term business growth.

3. Preparing for the Journey Ahead

Embrace Continuous Learning: Stay informed about industry trends, new methodologies, and evolving client needs.

Cultivate a Growth Mindset: View challenges as opportunities to improve and refine your consulting practice.

Celebrate Your Progress: Acknowledge milestones and small wins to maintain motivation and confidence.

EXERCISE: NEXT STEPS ACTION PLAN

Step 1: Outline Your Immediate Next Steps

Identify the immediate steps you need to take to start your consulting journey. These might include finalising your business plan, setting up your business legally, or reaching out to potential clients.

Step 2: Set Short-Term and Long-Term Goals

Establish clear short-term (next 3 months) and long-term (next 12 months) goals for your consulting business. Be specific about what you want to achieve, such as acquiring your first client, reaching a certain income level, or building a professional website.

Step 3: Identify Resources and Support

List the resources, tools, or support you will need to achieve your goals. This could include software, courses, mentorship, or financial resources.

Step 4: Develop a Success Mindset

Write down affirmations or success statements that reinforce your commitment and confidence in your consulting journey. For example: "I am capable of building a successful consulting business," or "I will take consistent action towards my goals."

Step 5: Reflect on Potential Challenges

Anticipate potential challenges you might face and outline strategies for overcoming them. Consider how staying connected to your 'why' and leveraging your network can help you navigate these challenges.

Step 6: Commit to Your Path Forward

Write a commitment statement that summarises your decision to move forward with consulting. Include your key goals, your motivations, and the first action you will take. Keep this statement visible as a daily reminder of your commitment to your consulting journey.

CONCLUSION

Congratulations on reaching the end of this book and taking the time to thoughtfully consider whether solo consulting is the right path for you.

Your journey through these chapters has been one of exploration, reflection, and self-discovery. As you stand at this crossroads, it's important to feel confident and empowered in whichever decision you make.

In this conclusion, we will recap the key takeaways from each part of the book, outline actionable steps for those ready to proceed with consulting and for those who are still undecided, and offer encouragement for the journey ahead—no matter which path you choose.

SUMMARY OF KEY TAKEAWAYS

Throughout this book, we have explored the multifaceted decision of whether to pursue solo consulting. Here's a recap of the main points from each part to reinforce the insights that will help you make an informed choice:

Part 1: Understanding Solo Consulting

We began by examining what solo consulting entails, including rewards, challenges, common myths and misconceptions, and how consulting compares to traditional employment. This foundation helped you understand the realities of consulting and set the stage for deeper exploration.

Key Insight: Consulting offers independence, variety, and the potential for higher earnings but also involves managing income variability, client relationships, and the full responsibility of running your own business.

Part 2: Self-Assessment: Are You Ready for Consulting?

In this part, we guided you through a detailed self-assessment to evaluate your personal and professional readiness for consulting. We explored factors such as your skill set, mindset, risk tolerance, and lifestyle fit.

Key Insight: Understanding your strengths, identifying areas for improvement, and assessing your risk tolerance are crucial steps in determining whether consulting aligns with your personality, goals, and lifestyle.

Part 3: Exploring the Market and Identifying Your Niche

We delved into the importance of finding your unique value proposition and understanding market demand for your expertise. This part emphasised the significance of niche selection and the need for adaptability in a dynamic consulting landscape.

Key Insight: A well-chosen niche that aligns with your skills and market demand is key to standing out in the consulting world. Flexibility and continuous learning enable you to pivot and refine your focus as needed.

Part 4: Decision-Making: Is Solo Consulting Right for You?

This part provided frameworks and reflective exercises to help you weigh the pros and cons of consulting based on your individual circumstances. We discussed setting realistic expectations, listening to your intuition, seeking mentorship, and making a confident decision.

Key Insight: Combining rational analysis with intuitive reflection allows you to make decisions that align with your deeper goals and values. Seeking advice and mentorship can provide additional clarity and support as you make your choices.

Part 5: Preparing for the Transition (Without Going Too Deep)

Finally, we discussed the initial steps to prepare for a transition into consulting, including creating a preliminary transition plan, building confidence and resilience, leveraging your network and resources, and staying connected to your 'why'.

Key Insight: A thoughtful transition plan that incorporates mindset shifts, financial preparation, and the leveraging of existing resources can ease your entry into consulting. Staying connected to your core motivations will guide you through uncertainties and challenges.

ACTION STEPS AND NEXT MOVES

Whether you are ready to move forward with consulting or are still undecided, here are some actionable steps to help you take the next steps based on your decision:

For Those Who Are Ready to Proceed with Consulting:

1. **Create a Detailed Business Plan:** Develop a comprehensive business plan that outlines your vision, services, target market, pricing strategy, marketing approach, and financial projections.
2. **Set Up Your Consulting Business:** Establish your business infrastructure, including legal setup, branding, online presence, and financial systems. Ensure you have all necessary registrations, licences, and a professional image.
3. **Start Networking and Marketing:** Leverage your existing network and begin marketing your consulting services. Reach out to contacts, join industry groups, and actively promote your expertise to attract clients.

4. **Secure Your First Clients:** Focus on acquiring your initial clients through referrals, pilot projects, or strategic outreach. Early wins will build your confidence and provide valuable experience.

5. **Invest in Continuous Learning:** Stay ahead of industry trends, enhance your skills, and remain adaptable. Continuous learning will keep you competitive and position you as a trusted expert in your field.

For Those Who Are Still Undecided:

1. **Continue Exploring Part-Time or Small Projects:** Experiment with consulting on a part-time basis or through small projects while maintaining your current employment. This low-risk approach allows you to gain experience and assess your readiness.

2. **Seek Additional Guidance and Mentorship:** Connect with experienced consultants or mentors who can offer insights, advice, and perspectives on your decision. Hearing real-world experiences can provide clarity.

3. **Revisit Your Self-Assessment:** Reflect on your personal and professional readiness for consulting. Consider whether there are specific areas that need further development or exploration before making a decision.

4. **Stay Connected to Your Why:** Regularly revisit the motivations behind your interest in consulting. Reflect on how consulting aligns with your goals and whether it continues to feel like the right fit for your future.

5. **Give Yourself Time:** Making a career decision is a process, not a race. Allow yourself the necessary time and space to explore your options thoroughly and without pressure.

ENCOURAGEMENT FOR THE JOURNEY AHEAD

No matter which path you choose—whether stepping into solo consulting or continuing in your current career trajectory—both choices are valid and valuable. The journey of self-discovery and decision-making you've undertaken is a significant achievement in itself. Embrace the clarity you've gained and trust that your path will continue to unfold as it is meant to.

For Those Choosing Consulting: Embrace the adventure of consulting with confidence and enthusiasm. Remember that challenges are part of the journey, but so are growth, learning, and the opportunity to make a meaningful impact. Trust in your abilities, stay connected to your why, and approach each day with resilience and a commitment to your vision. The consulting world is dynamic and rewarding, and with your unique skills and motivations, you have the potential to thrive.

For Those Continuing in Their Current Career: If you've decided that consulting isn't the right move for you at this time, celebrate the clarity and insight you've gained through this process. Your decision to continue on your current path is equally powerful and valid. Use the self-awareness you've developed to make intentional choices in your career, pursue growth opportunities, and stay true to your values and goals. The skills and insights you've explored will continue to serve you well, whatever path you take.

FINAL THOUGHTS

Your professional journey is uniquely yours, and every step you take is an opportunity to learn, grow, and make choices that align with your true self. Whether you are stepping into consulting or choosing another direction, trust that you have the wisdom, courage, and resilience to navigate your path with purpose and fulfilment.

Thank you for joining me on this journey of exploration and reflection. May your decision be guided by clarity, confidence, and a deep connection to your why. Here's to the next chapter of your professional journey—wherever it may lead.

ABOUT THE AUTHOR

Phil Charles has experience in government, consulting, and academia, including over 20 years as a solo consultant. He is particularly interested in helping technical professionals become self-employed, and sharing the lessons he learned the hard way!

GOING SOLO ACADEMY

The Academy advises technical professionals on how to become a (better) solo consultant. Becoming a solo consultant is an exciting journey filled with opportunities for personal growth, professional development, and financial success.

However, starting a consulting business also presents its own set of challenges. It requires strategic planning, effective marketing, strong client relationships, and continuous learning and adaptation. You will need to differentiate yourself in a competitive market, manage projects effectively, and deliver high-quality services that meet your clients' needs. That's where the Going Solo Academy comes in.

Sign up to receive the newsletter at https://goingsolo.substack.com

OTHER BOOKS BY THE AUTHOR

"Formal education will make you a living; self-education will make you a fortune."

Jim Rohn. 1930-2009. Author and Motivational Speaker

———

Series: Essential Career Skills for Technical Professionals

Master Your Focus Today: *Learn How to Focus Better, Identify Your Distractions, and Organize Your Week.*

Master the Habits of Effective People: *Transformative Daily Practices for High Achievement to Align Your Professional Life.*

The Attention Architect: *Techniques to Boost Productivity and Build Better Habits.*

Why it Matters: *Fuelling Your Technical Success with Purpose.*

The Guide to Accelerating Your Career: *Actionable Strategies, Tips and Resources.*

How to Do the Hard Things: *Learn How to Win Over Procrastination and Get Things Done*

Focus and Energy Made Easy: *Natural Strategies for All-Day Performance Without Crashes*

My Books: https://mybook.to/philcharles

———